A hand to hold,
an opinion to reject

Other Cathy Books From Andrews, McMeel & Parker

Thin thighs in thirty years
Wake me up when I'm a size 5
Men should come with instruction booklets
A mouthful of breath mints and no one to kiss
Another Saturday night of wild and reckless abandon
Eat your way to a better relationship

A hand to hold, an opinion to reject

A  Collection

by Cathy Guisewite

Andrews, McMeel & Parker
A Universal Press Syndicate Affiliate
Kansas City • New York

8

WE'RE CALLING HER "ZENITH", CATHY.

"ZENITH"?

"ZENITH": THE PEAK! THE BEST! THE ULTIMATE! THE PINNACLE OF EXCELLENCE!

IT'S A NAME THAT SUMS UP THE VISION UPON WHICH OUR WHOLE GENERATION WAS FOUNDED!

"ZENITH": THE TV SET.

I THINK IT'S TERRIBLE WHEN PEOPLE GIVE THEIR BABY A HYPHENATED LAST NAME LIKE THAT, CATHY.

I DO TOO, MOM.

YOU DO??

IT'S TERRIBLE! THEY ALWAYS PUT THE MAN'S NAME LAST.

WHY CAN'T THEY EVER PUT THE WOMAN'S NAME LAST? WHY CAN'T THE WOMAN BE IN THE "REAL LAST NAME" POSITION, AND THE MAN IN THE PATRONIZED MIDDLE SPOT?!!

WHY DO CHILDREN ONLY AGREE WITH YOU WHEN THEY'RE ON THEIR WAY TO SOMETHING WORSE?

IS THIS A GIFT OR IS IT FOR YOU?

FOR ME? ALL THAT?? OH, NO. HA, HA. NO!

MY BEST FRIEND JUST HAD A BABY. IT'S A GIFT!

WE'RE GOOD FRIENDS OF THE FAMILY. WE'RE BOTH GETTING GIFTS.

YES. GIFTS. GIFTS FOR THE RELATIVES! GIFT-WRAPPED CHOCOLATES FOR THE RELATIVES!!

HERE'S TO YOU, AUNT CHARLENE.

DITTO, AUNT CATHY.

"MOST NEWBORNS HAVE A 5-MINUTE ATTENTION SPAN FOR FLASH CARDS."

ANDREA, ZENITH IS ONLY TWO WEEKS OLD!

ZENITH HAS A CURIOUS, RECEPTIVE MIND! WHY SHOULD I SIT HERE GOO-ING SENSELESSLY WHEN I COULD BE TEACHING HER SOMETHING?!

LOOK, ZENITH! THIS IS SIMONE DE BEAUVOIR... THIS IS THE MONA LISA... THIS IS...IS...OOH, YOU'RE SO CUTE!!

...GOOGLY GOOGLY GA-GA GOOGLY....

..."MOST PARENTS HAVE A 9-SECOND ATTENTION SPAN"....

LUKE'S BUSY CHANGING ZENITH'S DIAPER.

ARE YOU USING CLOTH OR DISPOSABLE?

CLOTH DIAPERS ARE MADE OF REUSABLE, NATURAL FIBER. DISPOSABLE DIAPERS ARE SYNTHETIC, NON-BIODEGRADABLE POLLUTANTS!

THERE'S ONLY ONE CHOICE AN ENVIRONMENTALLY AWARE COUPLE CAN MAKE, CATHY.

BUY DISPOSABLE AND SEND A CONTRIBUTION TO GREENPEACE!!

I WANT US ALL TO LOOK SHARP FOR THE MEETING MONDAY, CATHY. KNOW WHAT I MEAN?

SURE, MR. PINKLEY.

MEN ARE EXPECTED TO THROW ON A SUIT FROM 1978. WOMEN ARE EXPECTED TO WEAR A STUNNING NEW OUTFIT.

TO "LOOK SHARP," A MAN HAS TO BRUSH HIS TEETH. A WOMAN HAS TO SPEND HOURS SHOPPING AND GETTING HER HAIR DONE, NAILS DONE AND MAKEUP DONE!!

...WHEN MAY I BEGIN?

11

7:00 AM.: TENSE. ANXIOUS. I EAT MY 150-CALORIE LUNCH AND TWO CANDY BARS ON THE WAY TO THE OFFICE.

12:00 NOON: HURRIED AND HASSLED. I DRIVE THROUGH THE "DRIVE-THRU" FOR A CHEESEBURGER AND FRIES.

8:00 P.M.: TIRED AND DEFENSELESS. I HAVE A BURRITO ON THE WAY TO THE CLEANERS... A DOVE BAR ON THE WAY TO AEROBICS...AND HALF A BAG OF GROCERIES ON THE WAY HOME FROM THE STORE.

THE SUMMER OF '86: 90¢ A GALLON AND THREE POUNDS TO THE MILE.

EVERY YEAR I SEE YOU BUY ANOTHER PAIR OF WHITE PANTS AND THEN I NEVER SEE YOU WEAR THEM, CATHY.

WHAT HAPPENS? DO YOU GAIN TOO MUCH WEIGHT? GET TOO INSECURE? DO YOU CHANGE YOUR MIND AND RETURN THEM?

WHERE DO THEY ALL GO??

LET'S JUST SAY WE ALL HAVE A FEW SKELETONS IN THE CLOSET, MOM....

...AND MINE ARE ALL WEARING WHITE PANTS.

YOU REALLY HAVE TO GET THIS REPORT IN, CATHY.

I KNOW. I JUST WANT TO CLEAR A SPACE ON MY DESK FIRST...

...OH. LOOK AT THE DUST. HOLD ON. I'LL JUST WIPE OFF THE DUST...

...AND PUT AWAY THESE FILES ...AND VACUUM UNDER THE CHAIR... AND SORT OUT THIS DRAWER... AND...HOLD ON....

INSIDE EVERY EXECUTIVE THERE'S A CLEANING PERSON SCREAMING TO GET OUT.

HOW ARE WE DOING?

GREAT! I ACTUALLY WROTE PART OF A PRESENTATION WITHOUT THE HELP OF ANY CHOCOLATE!

FITNESS COUNSELOR

I WORE MY SWIMSUIT ONCE WITHOUT CONSOLING MYSELF WITH PIE...AND TWICE IN JULY I'VE DRIVEN PAST FROZEN YOGURT WITHOUT STOPPING!

YOUR RIGHT CALF GREW 3/4."

I DON'T MAKE THE KIND OF PROGRESS YOU CAN MEASURE WITH A TAPE.

TNESS ELOR

"DEAR MIDLAND HIGH SCHOOL GRADUATE... IT'S REUNION TIME!"

"WE'VE FOUND OUR CAREERS, OUR CALLINGS, OUR SPOUSES, OURSELVES, OUR POLITICS, AND OUR RELIGIONS."

"PLEASE JOIN YOUR CLASS IN ACCEPTING ITS BIGGEST CHALLENGE YET: FINDING SUMMER CLOTHES IN JULY."

HIGH SCHOOL REUNION

SUNDRESS! I MUST HAVE A SUNDRESS FOR MY HIGH SCHOOL REUNION!

HOW ABOUT THIS NICE TWEEDY SPORT COAT?

WOOL

COATS

NEW'S FALL ARRIVAL

WHERE ARE THE SUMMER CLOTHES?! I KNOW YOU HAVE SUMMER CLOTHES BACK THERE!!

BACK WHERE?

COATS

WOOL

WINTER

BAM BAM

FALL SWEATER

BACK THERE! BACK IN THE SECRET LITTLE ROOM WHERE ALL THE SALESCLERKS HIDE!

WINTER

FALL

GET AHOLD OF YOURSELF, MISS! SALESCLERKS IN THIS FINE STORE DO NOT HIDE IN A "SECRET LITTLE ROOM" FILLED WITH SUMMER CLOTHES!!

WINTER

AHEM... SORRY....

THAT'S WHERE THE MANAGER HIDES.

DATS

WINTER

FALL SWEATERS

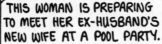

Panel 1: EACH FITNESS PROGRAM IS DE-SIGNED FOR THE GOALS OF THE INDIVIDUAL..... THIS WOMAN IS PREPARING TO GET INTO WHITE STRETCH PANTS IN AUGUST.
THIGH MACHINE.

Panel 2: THIS WOMAN IS PREPARING TO MEET HER EX-HUSBAND'S NEW WIFE AT A POOL PARTY.
BUST MACHINE

Panel 3: THIGH, BUST, REAR, WAIST & ARM MACHINE

Panel 4: OLYMPIC TRIALS? HIGH SCHOOL REUNION.

Panel 5: OH, HI. DID CATHY RUN TO HER TAN-NING BOOTH TO GET READY FOR HER HIGH SCHOOL REUNION? NO. SHE DIDN'T HAVE TIME.

Panel 6: CATHY HAD TO RESORT TO DO-ING WHAT PEOPLE DID BEFORE THERE WERE TANNING BOOTHS.

Panel 7: YOU DON'T MEAN... SEE FOR YOURSELF...

Panel 8: YAACK!! I'VE DYED MY LEGS ORANGE!! JUST LIKE THE GOOD OLD DAYS... INSTA-TAN

Panel 9: WANT TO BORROW AN OUTFIT OF MINE TO WEAR TO YOUR HIGH SCHOOL REUNION, CATHY?

Panel 10: ANDREA, I'M A SUCCESSFUL BUSINESSWOMAN. DO YOU ACTUALLY THINK I'D TRY TO IMPRESS MY EX-CLASSMATES WITH SOME-ONE ELSE'S CLOTHES?!!

Panel 11: SORRY.

Panel 12: MAY I BORROW YOUR HUSBAND AND BABY?

HERE I SIT: GODDESS OF THE TELEPHONE.

I COULD INVITE IRVING TO MY HIGH SCHOOL REUNION... OR MAX... OR ALEX... **MY WHIM**...

...IF I CALL ONE, WILL I WISH I'D CALLED ANOTHER? ...WOULD I RATHER GO ALONE ...I CAN'T DECIDE...I CAN'T COMMIT...I CAN'T MOVE...MY DIALING ARM IS FROZEN....

HERE I SIT: STATUE OF A GODDESS OF THE TELEPHONE.

READY FOR THE RAZOR? HA, HA!

THE RAZOR. HA, HA. WHY NOT?

YES. WHY **NOT** TURN HAIR I LOVE OVER TO A DRUG ADDICT WITH A RAZOR THE WEEK BEFORE MY HIGH SCHOOL REUNION?

GO AHEAD. BUZZ IT! FRIZZ IT! HACK IT! RUIN MY LIFE AND THEN SMILE AND SAY IT WILL "GROW OUT"! HA, HA!

HOW REFRESHING TO FIND SOMEONE SO SURE OF THE NEW STYLE SHE'S GOING TO GET!

snip.

AACK! TOO SHORT! TOO LAYER-Y! AACK! LET ME COUNT THE HAIRS ON THE FLOOR! WHERE'S A MIRROR?!

WHERE'S A LAWYER?! I'LL SUE! **NO TIP!!** TELL ME IT'S A NIGHTMARE! AACK! I'M FINISHED!!

I'M FINISHED.

FINISHED?! IT DOESN'T LOOK ANY DIFFERENT YET!

CATHY, YOU'VE DESTROYED YOUR HAIR... DYED YOUR LEGS ORANGE... AND SHAMED YOURSELF IN FIVE STORES PREPARING FOR THIS EVENT...

"PANT PANT"

...AND FOR WHAT? WHY DO YOU EVEN CARE ABOUT SEEING YOUR OLD HIGH SCHOOL GRADUATING CLASS??

IT'S JUST SOMETHING I HAVE TO DO, ANDREA.

I WANT TO JOURNEY BACK TO MY HOMETOWN AND STRANGLE THE PERSON WHO ORGANIZED THE REUNION.

WOMAN WAKING UP REMEMBERING A DATE SHE SHOULDN'T HAVE HAD:

NO...

WOMAN WAKING UP REMEMBERING A PIE SHE SHOULDN'T HAVE HAD:

NO...

WOMAN WAKING UP REMEMBERING A PHONE CALL SHE SHOULDN'T HAVE HAD:

NO...

WOMAN WAKING UP REMEMBERING A HAIRCUT SHE SHOULDN'T HAVE HAD:

NO! NO! NO! AACK! NO!!!!

GROW! GROW!! I BEG YOU! PLEASE GROW!

POINK! POINK! POINK! POINK!

NO! NOT YOU! NOT THE LEGS! NO! SHRINK! SHRINK!!!

BOING BOING BOING BOING BOING

PLOOP

BOING BOING BOING

AAACK!! NOT THE TOP! I DIDN'T WANT THE TOP TO SHRINK!!

SELF-IMAGING: TRIED BY MANY... ...MASTERED BY FEW.

I WISH I COULD JUST HIDE IN THE PARKING LOT WITH A BUNCH OF CLOTHES... WATCH WHAT EVERYONE ELSE WEARS INTO THE REUNION... AND THEN GET DRESSED ACCORDINGLY.

THAT'S RIDICULOUS. WHAT DOES THE INVITATION SAY ABOUT WHAT TO WEAR?

THE USUAL: "IF CATHY WEARS SOMETHING DRESSY, EVERYONE ELSE IS TO COME IN JEANS. IF CATHY WEARS JEANS, DRESS FORMAL."

READY TO GO, CATHY?

READY.

I SHOULD HAVE WORN A DRESS.

MIDLAND HIGH REUNION

NO. MY BLUE SKIRT. MY BLUE SKIRT WOULD HAVE BEEN PERFECT. NO. MY TAN DRESS. DEFINITELY. MY TAN WOULD...

CATHY, WE'RE ALREADY HERE! WOULD YOU QUIT CHANGING YOUR MIND ABOUT WHAT YOU'RE WEARING?!!!

I SHOULD HAVE BROUGHT A DIFFERENT DATE. NO. I SHOULD HAVE COME ALONE. NO. I SHOULD HAVE....

REUNION

IS MY LIPSTICK PERFECT, IRVING?? ELLEN KIMBEL ALWAYS USED TO RIDICULE ME FOR TRYING TO WEAR LIPSTICK IN HIGH SCHOOL.

MIDLAND HIGH REUNION

WHY WOULD YOU WANT TO GO TALK TO A WOMAN WHO USED TO RIDICULE YOU, CATHY??

WHEN SOMEONE'S BEEN THAT PETTY, IT'S IMPORTANT TO FACE HER ONE LAST TIME.

ME

FOR WHAT??

I WANT TO SEE HOW FAT SHE'S GOTTEN.

IMAGINE HOW WE'VE ALL PROGRESSED SINCE WE WERE GIRLS IN HIGH SCHOOL...

MIDLAND HIGH REUNION

WE'VE BECOME SUCCESSFUL, ESTABLISHED, CONFIDENT, WORLDLY, PROUD...

MIDLAND HIGH REUNION

WHO ELSE BUT SOMEONE WHO KNEW US THEN COULD APPRECIATE THE WOMEN WE'VE TURNED INTO?!

YOU LOOK EXACTLY LIKE YOUR MOTHER.

WHERE WERE **YOU** IN HIGH SCHOOL?

I WAS THE NERD YOU WOULDN'T TALK TO.

...BUT WHERE WERE **YOU** IN HIGH SCHOOL?

I WAS THE NERD YOU WOULDN'T TALK TO... ... BUT WHERE WERE **YOU**?!

I WAS THE NERD YOU WOULDN'T TALK TO.

...BUT WHERE WERE **YOU**??

PBLLTT!!

THE WONDER OF EVOLUTION: FROM A SCHOOL OF NERDS, A FLOCK OF GEEKS.

IS THIS YOUR HUSBAND, CATHY?

OH, NO. WE'RE NOT MARRIED.

REUNION

HE'S SINGLE?!

SINGLE MAN?!

THERE'S A SINGLE MAN HERE??!

A SINGLE MAN! IN OUR AGE BRACKET! LEMME SEE! LEMME AT HIM! STAND BACK, I HAVE DIBS!

STILL WORRIED THAT YOU WON'T HAVE ANYONE TO TALK TO, SWEETIE?

20

ALL WE EVER CARED ABOUT IN HIGH SCHOOL WAS, "WILL I GET A DATE?"

YEAH...OR, "CAN I BORROW THE CAR?"

OR, "WHERE'S MY ALLOWANCE?"

ALL "ME, ME, ME."

HOW REWARDING TO FINALLY BE AT THE STAGE WHERE OUR CARES GO BEYOND OUR OWN LIVES TO THE FAR MORE UNIVERSAL QUESTIONS...

HOW DID BOBBY EWING GET IN THAT SHOWER ??!

SHE SAID, "YOU CAN'T GO OUT IN A SKIRT THAT TIGHT!"...LIKE I'M STILL A KID!!

YEAH, HA, HA! MINE DOES THAT, TOO!

I THINK MINE WOULD ACTUALLY CALL THE POLICE IF I WEREN'T HOME BY MIDNIGHT!

I KNOW, HA, HA! THEY'RE ALL THE SAME!

YEAH....HA, HA!......HERE. I HAVE A PICTURE OF LITTLE JENNIFER RIGHT HERE!

OH, DEAR.

THEY'RE TALKING ABOUT THEIR DAUGHTERS. I WAS TALKING ABOUT MY MOTHER.

I JUST SAW RICKY, CATHY.

RICKY?? RICKY'S HERE??

ALL YOU COULD SAY WHEN YOU HEARD HIS NAME IN HIGH SCHOOL WAS, "HOW DOES MY HAIR LOOK?? HOW DOES MY HAIR LOOK??"

ISN'T IT GREAT THAT YOU CAN FACE HIM TODAY WITH MORE ON YOUR MIND THAN "HOW DOES MY HAIR LOOK?"!

YEAH...

HOW DO MY WRINKLES LOOK?

22

MY HIGH SCHOOL REUNION BROUGHT BACK SO MANY MEMORIES...RIDING MY BIKE TO McCANDLESS BOOKSTORE TO LOOK AT ALL THE NEW CARDS AND BOOKS AND GIFTS...

...STOPPING AT SWANSON'S FOR CANDY...GOING TO NUGENTS FOR A SODA...WANDERING AROUND HANSEN'S DEPARTMENT STORE...CURTIS BAKERY...LEMPKE'S BOOTERY...CITY DAIRY ICE CREAM...

THESE ARE MY RICHEST MEMORIES, ANDREA...MY FOUNDATION...IT'S WHO I AM...WHERE I CAME FROM...IT'S EVERYTHING I CARE ABOUT...IT'S..IT'S...

IT'S FOOD AND SHOPPING.

...FOOD AND SHOPPING....

CATHY, WILL YOU...

THAT DOES IT. I CAN'T WORK WITH ALL THESE INTERRUPTIONS.

FROM NOW ON, NO ONE IS TO WALK THROUGH THIS DOOR! NO ONE IS TO KNOCK ON, OPEN OR WALK THROUGH THIS DOOR! NO EXCEPTIONS! THIS DOOR STAYS CLOSED!!!

SLAM

I HAVE TO GO TO THE BATHROOM.

I THOUGHT YOUR WEIRD HAIRDO WOULD GO AWAY AFTER YOUR HIGH SCHOOL REUNION, CATHY.

NO SUCH LUCK, CHARLENE.

MY SLIM NEW SHAPE DISAPPEARED...MY BEAUTIFUL NAILS ARE GONE FOREVER... ...ALL IMPROVEMENTS INSTANTLY VANISHED.

ONLY THE WEIRD, HORRIBLE HAIRDO IS STILL WITH ME.

THE ONES YOU HOPE YOU NEVER HEAR FROM AGAIN ARE THE ONES WHO NEVER LOSE YOUR ADDRESS.

HOW BAD IS IT, ANDREA? IT'S BAD, CATHY.

MY MOTHER SAYS IT'S CUTE.

YOUR MOTHER WOULD SAY A GARBAGE CAN ON YOUR HEAD WAS CUTE.

NO MATTER HOW RIDICULOUS THE REST OF THE WORLD THINKS YOU LOOK, YOUR MOTHER SAYS YOU'RE CUTE SO YOU'LL LOVE HER... IT'S JUST A TRICK YOUR MOTHER USES TO MAKE SURE YOU LOVE HER!

IT'S WORKING.

I HAVE A $200 SKIN CARE SYSTEM ON THE COUNTER AND I'M STANDING IN THE SHOWER WASHING MY FACE WITH DEODORANT SOAP.

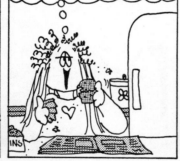

I'M SIX INCHES FROM A REFRIGERATOR OF FRESH VEGETABLES. HERE I SIT, EATING CHOCOLATE CHIP MUFFINS.

SURROUNDED BY NEWSPAPERS, FINE NOVELS AND CLASSICAL MUSIC, I PROP MY FEET ON THE COLLECTED WORKS OF SHAKESPEARE AND WATCH "THE LOVE CONNECTION".

PERFECTION IS WITHIN MY REACH, BUT JUST SLIGHTLY OUT OF MY GRASP.

YOUR HAIR IS ALL FLATTENED DOWN AND BACK TO NORMAL, CATHY. HOW IS THAT POSSIBLE?!

LET'S JUST SAY THAT IN A WORLD WHERE BOBBY EWING CAN COME BACK TO LIFE, ANYTHING'S POSSIBLE.

LET'S JUST SAY THAT IF FALLON COULD SHOW UP IN DENVER WITH A NEW FACE, I CAN BE HERE WITH NEW HAIR.

LET'S JUST SAY THAT IN 1986, IN THE WIDE SCREEN OF LIFE, WE ALL MAKE OUR OWN LITTLE REALITIES, CHARLENE...

LET'S JUST SAY THAT SOMEONE CASHED IN HER IRA ON A BATHROOM FULL OF HAIR SPRAY.

THANK YOU, MOTHER.

29

Row 1

LUKE AND I WILL BE LEAVING ZENITH WITH YOU FOR EXACTLY TWO HOURS. WE'LL HAVE A CELLULAR PHONE WITH US AT ALL TIMES, AND WE'RE BOTH WEARING BEEPERS.

I PROGRAMMED THE COMPUTER TO ELECTRONICALLY TRACK OUR CAR, WITH ONE-DIGIT DIALING FOR EVERY HOME BETWEEN HERE AND THE RESTAURANT.

WE'LL CHECK IN EVERY HALF-HOUR. IF YOU DON'T ANSWER BY THE THIRD RING, WE PUSH THIS BUTTON, WHICH INSTANTANEOUSLY SENDS THE PARAMEDICS, IN-LAWS, AND, OF COURSE, OUR OWN SWAT TEAM.

TWEET!

ARE YOU SURE YOU WANT TO GO OUT?

OH, YES! WE NEED AN EVENING TO JUST RELAX.

Row 2

SHE'S GOING TO START WAILING THE SECOND WE LEAVE, CATHY.

NO, SHE WON'T. MOMMY TOLD HER ALL ABOUT TONIGHT.

SHE'S GOING TO START WAILING THE SECOND WE LEAVE.

NO, SHE WON'T. MOMMY'S BIG GIRL WON'T WAIL, WILL SHE? NO!

WAAA!!

SHE STARTED WAILING THE SECOND WE LEFT.

WAAA!! COME TO MAMA!!

Row 3

WAVE BYE BYE, ZENITH!

AACK! I CAN'T LEAVE MY BABY!

SEE THE FUNNY FACE MOMMY'S MAKING? BYE BYE, FUNNY MOMMY!

LET ME GO, LUKE! I CAN'T LEAVE MY BABY!!

AACK! MY BABY! I'M HERE, BABY!!

WAAAH!!

WE CAN'T LEAVE NOW, LUKE. SHE'S TOO UPSET.

YOU COULDN'T LEAVE ZENITH FOR **TWO HOURS** TONIGHT, ANDREA?? WHAT'S HAPPENED TO YOU?!

OVER-BONDING.

OVERBONDING?

THE PARENT GETS SO ATTACHED TO THE BABY THAT SHE TOTALLY DISTORTS WHAT MIGHT HAPPEN IF SHE ISN'T WITH HER 24 HOURS A DAY.

IT'S IRRATIONAL, HYSTERICAL BEHAVIOR THAT I CAN'T BELIEVE I GAVE IN TO. ZENITH IS AS STRONG AND HEALTHY AS A TWO-MONTH-OLD CAN BE!

WHY DON'T YOU JUST GO CHANGE CLOTHES?

WHAT IF SHE STARTS WALKING WHILE I'M IN THE BEDROOM??!!

I'VE LOVED MY TIME AT HOME WITH ZENITH, CATHY. WE MAKE HOME VIDEOS...

...DRESS HER IN A LITTLE FRENCH SWEATSUIT...DO HER BABY EXERCISE VIDEO...PLAY WITH STUFFED REPRODUCTIONS OF 17TH-CENTURY SCULPTURE ...STUDY MUSIC THEORY ON HER COMPUTER...AND SOMETIMES JUST ROCK IN THE ITALIAN LACQUERED ROCKER.

...STILL, THE DAY COMES WHEN A WOMAN REALIZES SHE JUST HAS TO GO BACK TO WORK.

I KNOW... IT'S TIME TO TEACH ZENITH INDEPENDENCE.

OUR VISA BILL CAME IN.

HOW CAN I GO BACK TO WORK WHEN THERE'S SO MUCH TO TEACH ZENITH?

DO YOU REALLY THINK A TWO-MONTH-OLD CAN LEARN?

OH, YES!! UNDER THAT BABY FACE HER BRAIN CELLS ARE MULTIPLYING AT A SPEED THAT WON'T BE MATCHED FOR THE REST OF HER LIFE!!

PBLTT!!

BY THE TIME ZENITH IS SIX MONTHS OLD, 50% OF HER TOTAL BRAIN GROWTH WILL HAVE OCCURRED...SHE **CRAVES** INTELLIGENT INPUT!!

PBLTTT!!

BABIES ARE NATURAL SCHOLARS.

PBLTT!

AND NATURAL TATTLETALES.

I'M BACK! I FINALLY DECIDED IT'S TIME FOR THIS NEW MOMMY TO EASE BACK INTO THE WORK FORCE!

HOW NICE FOR YOU.

I THINK I'D LIKE TO START A FEW HOURS A DAY... BUILD TO A 30-HOUR WEEK... OF COURSE GOING HOME TO NURSE OR BRINGING ZENITH HERE FOR LUNCH!

ISN'T THAT SWEET.

THEN MAYBE THE CHAIRMAN OF THE BOARD WILL COME SKIPPING DOWN THE HALL WITH BASKETS OF TOYS FOR **ALL** THE CHILDREN WHILE OUR CLIENTS SING LULLABYE DUETS IN THE RECEPTION AREA!!

SORRY. I WAS BEING A LITTLE UNREALISTIC. I'D LIKE TO COME BACK TO WORK.

WE GAVE AWAY YOUR JOB LAST MONTH.

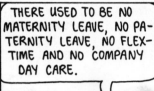

THERE USED TO BE NO MATERNITY LEAVE, NO PATERNITY LEAVE, NO FLEX-TIME AND NO COMPANY DAY CARE.

BUT WE PLEDGED TO CHANGE ALL THAT! TO PAVE THE WAY FOR THE NEXT GENERATION OF WOMEN!

WELL, HERE SHE IS! ZENITH! THE NEXT GENERATION OF WOMEN!

WE HAVE NO MATERNITY LEAVE, NO PATERNITY LEAVE, NO FLEX-TIME AND NO DAY CARE.

WE'RE NOT QUITE READY FOR YOU YET.

HOW COULD YOU GIVE MY JOB AWAY?!

COMPANIES AREN'T REQUIRED TO HOLD JOBS FOR WOMEN WHO TAKE TIME OFF TO HAVE BABIES, ANDREA.

THAT'S RIDICULOUS! 44% OF THE WHOLE LABOR FORCE IS WOMEN, AND 80% OF US WILL HAVE CHILDREN! THIS IS 1986!!

LET'S JUST SAY THIS COMPANY BELIEVES IN OLD-FASHIONED VALUES.

WHAT??

THEY FOUND SOMEONE WHO WOULD TAKE YOUR JOB FOR A 1950 SALARY.

EVERY INDUSTRIALIZED NATION IN THE WORLD PROVIDES MATERNITY LEAVE UP TO A YEAR EXCEPT **AMERICA**, WHERE A WOMAN CAN **LOSE** HER JOB FOR TAKING MORE THAN TWO WEEKS OFF TO GIVE BIRTH ??!!

AN UGLY EXAGGERATION. OFTEN WE GIVE HER THE JOB BACK, BUT JUST TAKE AWAY ALL SENIORITY...SOMETIMES WE GIVE BACK HER TITLE, BUT REMOVE ALL STATUS, AUTHORITY AND HOPE FOR ADVANCEMENT.

OF COURSE, WE'D MUCH RATHER **NOT** LET A NEW MOTHER GO.

WELL, THAT'S GOOD TO HEAR.

IF SHE QUITS ON HER **OWN**, WE CAN SKIP THE WHOLE SEVERANCE PAY FIASCO !

MOST WOMEN NEED THE INCOME OF A FULL-TIME JOB, BUT DAY CARE COSTS ALMOST AS MUCH AS THEY CAN EARN.

IF COMPANIES DON'T HELP WITH MATERNITY LEAVE OR CHILD CARE, IT'S HOPELESS.

IT'S LIKE SAYING ONLY RICH PEOPLE CAN HAVE CHILDREN !!

NO ONE'S SAYING ONLY RICH PEOPLE CAN HAVE CHILDREN.

THANK YOU.

ONLY RICH PEOPLE CAN HAVE JOBS.

IF THE "FAMILY AND MEDICAL LEAVE ACT" COULD REALLY GUARANTEE MATERNITY LEAVES, WHY AREN'T THERE BIG DEMONSTRATIONS FOR IT ?

BY WHOM, CATHY ?

THE PEOPLE MOST DESPERATE FOR THE BILL ARE SIMULTANEOUSLY RECOVERING FROM BIRTH, WORKING FULL TIME, CARING FOR A NEWBORN, **AND** DOING ALL THE SHOPPING, COOKING AND CLEANING FOR A HUSBAND AND ONE OR MORE OTHER CHILDREN ! WHO'S GOING TO DEMONSTRATE?

WHY DON'T THEY WRITE LETTERS ?

COULD YOU WRITE YOUR CONGRESSPERSON TONIGHT ?

YEAH...RIGHT AFTER I WHIP OFF A NOTE TO THE QUEEN OF ENGLAND.

35

THIS YEAR I'M REALLY GOING TO LOOK BEFORE I BUY FALL CLOTHES, CATHY!

ME TOO, MOM!

I WILL BUY NO FADS!

NO UNMATCHED SEPARATES!

NOTHING I HAVE TO HAND WASH!!

NOTHING I HAVE TO LOSE WEIGHT TO WEAR!!

...AAACK! THIS IS ADORABLE! I MUST HAVE THIS! I'LL LOSE WEIGHT! I'LL WASH IT! I'LL MATCH IT! I'LL TAKE IT!!

WHY DO YOU EVEN BOTHER WITH THE BIG PEP TALK?

IT'S SORT OF LIKE SINGING THE NATIONAL ANTHEM BEFORE A FOOTBALL GAME.

I KNOW EXACTLY HOW THIS COMPANY SHOULD BE RUN. NO ONE ASKS.

I KNOW PRECISELY WHAT THEY CAN DO WITH BANKS, INSURANCE COMPANIES, POLLUTION, THE ARMS RACE AND THE "NEW FALL SILHOUETTE." NO ONE ASKS.

I DON'T HAVE THE SLIGHTEST IDEA WHAT MY FUTURE WILL BE WITH IRVING, OR THE VAGUEST CLUE ABOUT HOW WE MIGHT MAKE IT WORK. EVERYONE ASKS.

PEOPLE ONLY LOOK IN THE CUPBOARDS THAT ARE A MESS.

IT'S FUNNY HOW WE WORRY ABOUT DIFFERENT PARTS OF OUR BODIES AT DIFFERENT TIMES OF OUR LIVES.

A BIGGER BUST! FLATTER REAR! ROUNDER REAR! SLIMMER LEGS! TEENSY WAIST!

NOW I LOOK AT MYSELF, AND IT ALL SEEMS KIND OF SILLY, MOM.

I KNOW, SWEETIE.

NOW I WANT SILICONE INJECTIONS IN THE SHOULDERS.

MAX IS GETTING MARRIED, MOM. LET'S SEE...THAT MAKES:
RICHARD: MARRIED
MARK: MARRIED
PAUL: ENGAGED
GRANT: ON THE BRINK...

YOU KEEP A MENTAL RECORD OF THE MARITAL STATUS OF EVERYONE YOU'VE EVER DATED, CATHY??

WHAT'S WRONG WITH THAT?

I'M SURPRISED YOU EVEN REMEMBER! YOU HAVEN'T SEEN SOME OF THOSE PEOPLE IN YEARS!

I GUESS IT IS SORT OF SILLY.

CROSS MAX OFF THE MASTER CHART, DEAR!

CRAIG JOEY
BRIAN TONY MARK
ROBERT OTTO EMER
LES PAUL BRAT
RICHARD JEFF TODD
CHRIS ALEX IRV
MAX

HOT LINE

Guisewite

CATHY, IF YOU LIKED MAX SO MUCH, WHY DIDN'T YOU PURSUE HIM WHEN YOU HAD THE CHANCE?

I THOUGHT THERE WAS PLENTY OF TIME, MOM.

YOU PROCRASTINATED?? ON SOMETHING LIKE THAT?!!

OH, LOOK WHO'S TALKING.

YOU PUT EVERYTHING OFF UNTIL LATER! MENDING... BILLS...SHOPPING...READING... NOTES...LOOK AROUND, MOM!

I SEE.

Guisewite

OUR DAUGHTER WILL NEVER MARRY OR BEAR CHILDREN BECAUSE I LET THE MAIL STACK UP ON THE COUNTER.

ALL WEEK IT SEEMED AS IF I WAS RUNNING IN THE WRONG DIRECTION.

EVERYONE WAS HERE... I WAS OVER THERE....

NOW IT'S THE WEEKEND, AND I CAN FINALLY COLLECT MYSELF ALL IN ONE PLACE.

AT LAST...I'M IN SINK WITH THE REST OF THE WORLD.

Guisewite

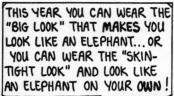

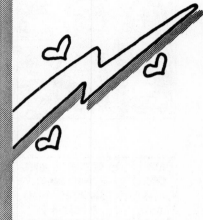

41

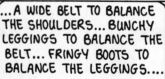

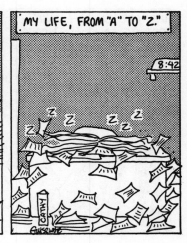

45

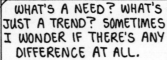

IT'S ALMOST IMPOSSIBLE TO KNOW WHERE OUR OWN INSTINCTS LEAVE OFF AND PEER PRESSURE BEGINS, CHARLENE.

I KNOW, CATHY.

WHAT'S A NEED? WHAT'S JUST A TREND? SOMETIMES I WONDER IF THERE'S ANY DIFFERENCE AT ALL.

YEAH...YOU'RE STARTING TO WONDER IF YOU WANT A BABY JUST SO YOU'LL FIT IN?

WORSE. I'M HAVING A BIOLOGICAL URGE TO BUY CHUNKY SILVER JEWELRY.

I HATE RETURNING THINGS, MOM.

WE ALL HATE RETURNING THINGS, CATHY, BUT IT HAS TO BE DONE.

I HATE FACING THE SALESPERSON. I NEVER KNOW WHAT TO SAY.

JUST TELL THE TRUTH.

REASON FOR RETURN?

I WANTED AN EXCUSE TO GO SHOPPING AGAIN.

YOU'LL LET ME FIX YOU UP ON A BLIND DATE?!!

SHHH!!

I THINK BLIND DATES ARE GREAT.

YOU DO?

ABSOLUTELY! IT MEANS YOU'RE FINALLY READY FOR A DATE THAT'S BEEN SELECTED BY SOMEONE WHO'S REALLY SENSITIVE TO YOUR NEEDS.

I'M READY FOR A DATE THAT I CAN BLAME ON SOMEONE ELSE.

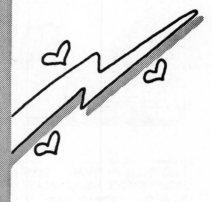

47

48

49

WHAT'S YOUR GENERAL ORIENTATION TOWARD LIFE, DEAN?

HUH?

WHAT'S YOUR BASIC NATURE? WHAT DO YOU RESPOND TO?

HUH?

WHAT'S THE ESSENCE OF YOUR PERSONALITY AND RELATIONSHIP TO OTHERS?

HUH?

IT'D BE SO MUCH EASIER IF I COULD JUST ASK WHAT HIS SIGN IS....

CHARLENE, MY BLIND DATE WAS...

I'M SORRY. HE USED TO BE CUTER! HE USED TO BE NICER!

NO, WAIT! I HAD A GREAT TIME!

IT'S NOT MY FAULT! I HAVEN'T SEEN HIM! I'M INNOCENT!!

WE'RE CRAZY ABOUT EACH OTHER.

YOU'RE CRAZY ABOUT EACH OTHER??

WAIT! NOT THAT CRAZY! JUST OK! FAIR! SO-SO.

I KNEW HIM FIRST! I WANT HIM BACK! I HAVE DIBS!

PERSON GREETING A BLINKING LIGHT, INDICATING THERE ARE MESSAGES:

"Blink" Blink Blink

PERSON GREETING A SOLID, STUNNED BEAM OF LIGHT, INDICATING NO MESSAGES:

PERSON GREETING NO LIGHT AT ALL, INDICATING SHE FORGOT TO TURN THE MACHINE ON.

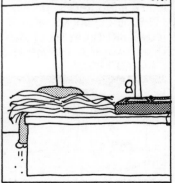

THOSE OF US WHO DON'T LOOK LIKE OUR PETS ARE STARTING TO LOOK LIKE OUR ANSWERING MACHINES.

THERE'S NO REASON A WOMAN CAN'T CALL A MAN AFTER THE FIRST DATE, CATHY.

SURE...I COULD HAVE CALLED RIGHT AFTER THE DATE, BUT HE SPECIFICALLY SAID HE WANTED TO CALL ME.

BY THE TIME I WAITED LONG ENOUGH TO GIVE HIM A CHANCE TO CALL, IT WAS TOO LATE TO CALL HIM WITHOUT SEEMING TO BE ASKING WHAT HAPPENED.

NOW I CAN'T CALL HIM. HE'LL KNOW I'VE BEEN WAITING. I'LL SOUND TOO ANXIOUS. TOO NEEDY. NO. BEFORE WOULD HAVE BEEN PERFECT. NOW WOULD BE HUMILIATING. AACK. NO. IT'S TOO LATE. NO.

HOW LONG HAS IT BEEN?

THIRTY-SIX HOURS.

THIS BOOK SAYS THE WAY TO A MAN'S HEART IS TO LEARN TO SPEAK IN HIS "VISUAL, AUDITORY, OR FEELINGS-RELATED LOVE LANGUAGE," CATHY.

THIS BOOK SAYS MEN CAN'T RESIST A WOMAN WHO'S MASTERED THE "CRITICISM-PRAISE BALANCE"... THIS ONE SAYS YOU CAN MAKE THEM GO CRAZY WITH "THE FIVE KEYS TO ROMANTIC TENSION"....

CALL ME, DEAN! CALL ME! CALL ME! CALL ME!!

SMASH

THEY ALL KIND OF RUN TOGETHER WHEN YOU TRY TO PUT THEM INTO PRACTICE.

HE SAID HE'D CALL. HE NEVER CALLED. WHY? ONE BRAVE WOMAN GOES IN SEARCH OF THE ANSWER.

DID HE NEVER MEAN TO CALL AT ALL? DID HE MEAN TO CALL BUT CHANGE HIS MIND? ...HER MIND RACES, TRYING TO FUSE QUESTIONS WITH A CLEAR ARTICULATION OF JUST HOW MISERABLE THIS MAKES A WOMAN FEEL.

SHE STRUGGLES TO STAY COOL... COOL BUT THOROUGH... THOROUGH BUT INTENSE...REMEMBER ALL THE QUESTIONS...EXPRESS THE FEELINGS...KEEP THE DIGNITY... HER HEART FILLS... HER BRAIN IS POUNDING...SHE REACHES THE DOOR...

PBLTTT!

AACK!

...THE DIALOGUE BEGINS.

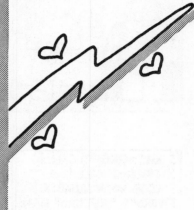

...WELL, THANKS. YOU MADE ME REALLY SEE HOW A WOMAN CAN FEEL WHEN A MAN SAYS HE'LL CALL AND THEN DOESN'T, CATHY.

YEAH... WELL, YOU REMINDED ME THAT MEN CAN BE INSECURE, TOO.

WHEN A WOMAN GIVES ME HER PHONE NUMBER LIKE THIS, I WILL NEVER AGAIN JUST STUFF IT IN A DRAWER!

AND I WON'T WAIT FOR THE MAN TO TAKE ACTION!

SO...UM... I'LL CALL YOU, CATHY..

AND I'LL CALL YOU, DEAN.

RIP RIP RIP

RIP RIP RIP

A ROOF OVER OUR HEADS... A SAFE PLACE TO SLEEP... WARM CLOTHES TO WEAR... HOPE FOR THE FUTURE...

WHEN YOU HAVE A TINY NEW BABY LIKE ZENITH, YOU REALIZE IT ISN'T ENOUGH TO JUST GIVE THANKS FOR THE FOOD ON THE TABLE.

SPLASH PLOP WHEE SPLAT BAM BAM!

NOW WE GIVE THANKS FOR THE FOOD UNDER THE TABLE.

WHEN THANKSGIVING IS OVER, IT REALLY SEEMS AS IF WINTER HAS BEGUN.

THE AIR IS COLD, THE FIRST SNOW FALLS...

AND EVERYWHERE YOU GO, YOU START HEARING THOSE FAMILIAR WORDS....

AAACK! MY $100 BOOTS ARE GETTING WET!!!

MALL

LOT A

ARENT YOU GOING TO DO ALL YOUR CHRISTMAS SHOPPING BY CATALOGUE THIS YEAR, CATHY?

NO.

IT'S SO EFFICIENT!

ANDREA, DON'T YOU THINK YOU'RE MISSING THE WHOLE POINT?...THE WHOLE MAGICAL EXPERIENCE OF GOING OUT SHOPPING FOR YOUR LOVED ONES??!

WHY? BECAUSE I CAN'T TOUCH THE GIFTS I PICK OUT FOR PEOPLE?

YOU CAN'T TRY ON ANY CLOTHES.

HOW COULD YOU BLAB MY BLIND DATE STORY TO THE WHOLE BUILDING, CHARLENE??

I DON'T KNOW, CATHY.

I PRIDE MYSELF IN MY ABILITY TO RECEIVE AND DISTRIBUTE INFORMATION, BUT THIS ONE WENT OVER THE TOP.

I WHISPERED IT... HONED IT... ROUTED IT!... PEOPLE DON'T JUST KNOW THE STORY... ...BY 9:30 THIS MORNING MOST OF THE OFFICE COULD RE-ENACT YOUR ENTIRE LAST CONVERSATION!!!

I DON'T THINK CATHY MEANT IT AS A COMPLIMENT, CHARLENE.

OH.

WHAT'S IRVING BEEN DOING WHILE YOU'VE BEEN WORRYING ABOUT DEAN, CATHY?

I WISH I KNEW.

DOES HE GET CRAZY WITH JEALOUSY? DOES HE SNEAK AROUND WITH OTHER PEOPLE WHEN I SNEAK AROUND WITH OTHER PEOPLE? HOW WOULD I EVER FIND OUT??

THIS IS THE ONE THING MY RELATIONSHIP WITH IRVING HAS ALWAYS BEEN LACKING.

TRUST?

SPIES.

I CAN'T THINK OF ANYTHING TO GET FOR THE MEN ON MY LIST.

GO THROUGH WOMEN'S PERFUME, WOMEN'S COSMETICS, WOMEN'S JEWELRY, WOMEN'S PURSES, WOMEN'S HOSIERY, WOMEN'S HATS, WOMEN'S LUGGAGE, WOMEN'S BARRETTES, WOMEN'S SUNGLASSES, WOMEN'S SHOES, WOMEN'S BELTS, WOMEN'S LINGERIE, WOMEN'S SPORTSWEAR, WOMEN'S FORMAL WEAR AND YOU'LL SEE A LITTLE CORNER FOR THE MEN.

YOU HAVE 50 DEPARTMENTS FOR WOMEN AND ONE LITTLE CORNER FOR MEN ??

WE COULDN'T THINK OF ANYTHING, EITHER.

THIS 21-RANGE ANALOG TESTER MAKES A GREAT GIFT FOR THAT SPECIAL GUY!

THAT MAKES A GREAT GIFT ??

FOR HIM

THE 7-BAND EQUALIZER WITH 80-WATT BOOSTER IS ON SO MANY WISH LISTS!

YOU'RE KIDDING.

AND WHAT MAN DOESN'T DREAM OF OWNING A 5-TIER TACKLE BOX WITH DETACHABLE WORM BASKET ?!!

DID YOU GET MY CHRISTMAS PRESENT?

ONCE I FOUND OUT WHAT YOU'D WANT I DIDN'T LIKE YOU ANYMORE.

I'LL COME TO STAY AT YOUR HOUSE ON THE 23RD AND WILL LEAVE ON THE 26TH, MOM.

OH. SO SOON? YOU CAN'T STAY LONGER?

CATHY

I'M NOT EVEN THERE YET!

YOUR VISITS ARE ALWAYS SO SHORT.

CATH

MOM, YOU HAVE THREE WEEKS BEFORE I GET THERE. ...WE'LL TALK TWICE A DAY.. ...ARE YOU GOING TO DO THIS TO ME FORTY-TWO MORE TIMES BEFORE THE HOLIDAY BEGINS ?!!

WHY SAVE IT ALL FOR CHRISTMAS WHEN I HAVE THIS MUCH TO GIVE?

Guisewite

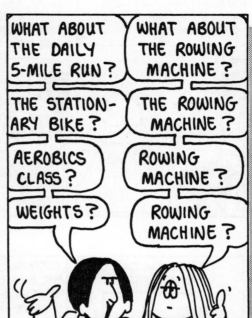

Panel 1: WELL, I SEE THE McPHERSONS HAVE GONE TO COMPUTERIZED ADDRESS LABELS ON THEIR PRE-PRINTED CHRISTMAS CARDS.

Panel 2: SO WHAT, MOM? IT JUST MEANS THEY HAVE A COMPUTER THIS YEAR.

Panel 3: CATHY, THE USE OF COMPUTERIZED ADDRESS LABELS SAYS MUCH MORE THAN "WE HAVE A COMPUTER"!

Panel 4: IT SAYS, "WE HAVE A COMPUTER AND SOMEONE IN OUR FAMILY UNDERSTOOD THE INSTRUCTION BOOK".

SHOW-OFFS!

Panel 5: A VIDEO TAPE? CERTAINLY. BETA, VHS OR 8 MILLIMETER? T120, 240, 360 OR L165, 500 OR 750? HGX? XHG? HIGH-GRADE HGX? EX? CHROME SUPER HG HIFI? HIFI STEREO? ESX-HIFI? DYNAMICRON ES-HG? OR EPITAXIAL? FOR THE SP, LP, SLP OR EP MODE?

Panel 6: MAYBE I'LL JUST GET AN AUDIO TAPE.

Panel 7: CERTAINLY. HIGH BIAS, NORMAL BIAS OR METAL? 46, 90 OR 60? TDK SA-X, AD-S, D, SA, MA-X OR HX-S?? SONY HF, HF-S, UX-S, UX-PRO, METAL-ES, UCX-60 OR LH-MAXIMA? BASF LH OR CHROMDIOXID EXTRA II? MAXELL XLII-S, UDS-II, XLI-S, OR MX-METAXIAL POSITION IEC, TYPEIV? UDS-I, XL-I, XL-II, UXHG

Panel 8: IT'S FINALLY HAPPENED... I CAN'T EVEN FIGURE OUT HOW TO BUY SOMETHING THAT'S TOTALLY BLANK.

Panel 9: "MERRY CHRISTMAS, BARB! HERE'S A LITTLE SOMETHING I GOT FOR..."..NO. TOO DEMEANING. "A BOX FOR BARB!.. HA, HA..."..NO. TOO GOOFY.

Panel 10: "THINKING OF YOU, BARB.."..NO. TOO NORMAL. "MY DEAREST BARB.."..TOO MUSHY.

Panel 11: "HI, BARB!"...NO. "FRIEND BARB...". NO. "HERE'S TO..." ...NO. "MERRIEST WI.." NO.

RIP RIP RIP RIP

Panel 12: "DEAR BARB, THERE WILL BE NO GIFT THIS YEAR. I USED UP MY WHOLE BOX OF CARDS ON YOU."

WHERE'S THE ACCOUNTING DEPARTMENT, CATHY?

THEY FIGURED NO ONE WOULD GET ANYTHING DONE SO THEY WENT HOME EARLY FOR CHRISTMAS.

CHRISTMAS IS STILL TEN DAYS AWAY!

YEAH... IT CREEPS UP EVERY YEAR.

PEOPLE USED TO START LEAVING EARLY ON CHRISTMAS EVE... THEN AT NOON ON THE 23RD... THEN AT 3:00 ON THE 22ND... AND NOW...

I'M GOING TO SPEAK TO THE MANAGEMENT SQUAD ABOUT THIS!!

THE MANAGEMENT SQUAD NEVER CAME BACK FROM THANKSGIVING.

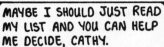

"TO BOB AND SUE"... WHAT HAVE THEY BEEN UP TO, CATHY?

WHO KNOWS, ANDREA?

THE ONLY TIME BOB AND SUE EVER THINK ABOUT ME IS WHEN THEY SEE MY NAME ON THEIR CHRISTMAS CARD LIST AND WONDER IF THIS IS THE YEAR TO CROSS ME OFF.

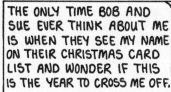

WHY WOULD YOU KEEP SENDING CHRISTMAS CARDS TO PEOPLE LIKE THAT??!

WE HAVE A LOT IN COMMON.

MAYBE I SHOULD JUST READ MY LIST AND YOU CAN HELP ME DECIDE, CATHY.

OK.

GUESS JEANS... REEBOK SNEAKERS... PERUVIAN HAND-LOOMED CAPE... OVERSIZED DENIM JACKET WITH EMBROIDERED INLAYS... ONYX STUD EARRINGS... ITALIAN LEATHER JUMPSUIT... PICTURE BOOK OF SOUTHWEST AMERICAN POTTERY....

OH, ANDREA! ANYTHING!! I WOULD LOVE ANY OF THOSE THINGS!!!

THIS IS THE LIST FOR OUR SIX-MONTH-OLD DAUGHTER.

OH.

WE HAVE YOU DOWN FOR A FRUITCAKE.

OF COURSE, ALL TOYS FOR MY BABY MUST BE 100% SAFE, TESTED AND WHOLESOME.

OF COURSE.

THEY MUST BE NON-TOXIC, NON-POLLUTING, NON-FLAMMABLE, NON-VIOLENT, STERILE, AND VACUUM SEALED IN THE ORIGINAL CARTON WITH A CLEAR LIST OF MATERIALS PRINTED ON THE BOX!!

YOUR GERM-FREE DAUGHTER IS SUCKING DIRT OFF THE CAR KEYS YOU DUG OUT OF THE BOTTOM OF YOUR PURSE AND THEN DROPPED ON THE FLOOR, ANDREA.

WHAT DO YOU HAVE THAT'S FAIRLY CLEAN?

"TRANSFORMER" TOYS ARE A VERY HOT ITEM! FOR LITTLE BOYS WE HAVE BATTLE TANKS THAT TRANSFORM INTO DEATH RAY LASER GUNS...BOMBER JETS THAT TRANSFORM INTO MINI-NUCLEAR WARHEADS....

...AND FOR LITTLE GIRLS WE HAVE KITCHENETTES THAT TRANSFORM INTO MAKEUP TRAYS!

YOUR "BOY TOYS" TRANSFORM INTO MURDER WEAPONS AND YOUR "GIRL TOYS" TRANSFORM INTO BEAUTY PRODUCTS?? ARE YOU OUT OF YOUR MINDS?! HAVE YOU TOTALLY LOST TOUCH?

MY CUSTOMER IS TRANSFORMING INTO A MONSTER.

NO BIGGIE. JUST TRANSFORM YOURSELF INTO A ROBOT.

BAM BAM BAM

WHAT DO YOU MEAN IT'S TOO LATE TO ORDER FROM A CATALOG FOR CHRISTMAS?? THIS IS THE UNITED STATES OF AMERICA!

FEDERAL EXPRESS IT! EXPRESS MAIL! EMERY! AIRBORNE! BLUE LABEL UPS! ZAP MAIL! SATELLITE TRANSMISSION!!

CHARTER A JET! HIRE A MESSENGER! BUT GET THAT PACKAGE DELIVERED BEFORE CHRISTMAS EVE!!!

THE '80s GIFT: A $15 WATCH WITH A $150 SHIPPING CHARGE.

MY BOYFRIEND HAS 4 WATCHES, 4 TELEPHONES, 6 RADIOS, 3 TV SETS, 5 TAPE PLAYERS, 4 CAMERAS...

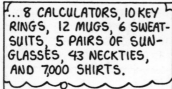

...8 CALCULATORS, 10 KEY RINGS, 12 MUGS, 6 SWEAT-SUITS, 5 PAIRS OF SUN-GLASSES, 43 NECKTIES, AND 7,000 SHIRTS.

I'VE QUIT LOOKING FOR SOMETHING UNIQUE AND AM TRYING TO FIND SOME-THING HE HAS LESS THAN THREE OF.

A SHIRT FOR DAD...SWEATER FOR MOM...GLOVES FOR ANDREA... A CAMERA..TOTE-BAG... WORKOUT TAPE... NECKLACE...WALLET...PHONE ...BOOK...ALBUM...COFFEE MAKER...STOCKING STUFFERS ...TABLE DECORATIONS....

...OK. A SHIRT FOR DAD... A SWEATER FOR MOM...

...OK, A PARKING SPACE. JUST GIVE ME A PARK-ING SPACE. ALL I WANT IS A PARKING SPACE!!

AS A RELATIONSHIP GOES ON, OUR EXPECTATIONS GET MORE REALISTIC.

WANT TO SEE WHAT I GOT IRVING FOR CHRISTMAS?

NO. IT'S ALL WRAPPED.

DON'T YOU WANT TO LOOK AT IT??

I DON'T MIND OPENING IT.

DON'T BE SILLY.

CATHY, GET HOLD OF YOURSELF!!

YOU'RE RIGHT. WITH ALL I HAVE TO DO, IT WOULD BE CRAZY TO STAND HERE WITH YOU AND UNWRAP THE ONE GIFT I HAVE READY!

...WHEN I CAN WAIT UNTIL YOU LEAVE AND DO IT IN PEACE.

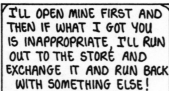

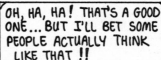

64

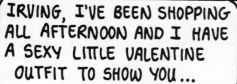

IRVING, I'VE BEEN SHOPPING ALL AFTERNOON AND I HAVE A SEXY LITTLE VALENTINE OUTFIT TO SHOW YOU...

AACK. I CAN'T BELIEVE I DID THAT... AACK! NOW HE'S COMING OVER !!

HE CAN'T SEE ME LIKE THIS! I LOOK RIDICULOUS! I LOOK LIKE A BIMBO! WHAT WAS I THINKING ???

I DON'T SEE ANYTHING DIF-FERENT, CATHY.

MEN HAVE NO IMAGINA-TION.

Guisewite

THE PROFESSIONAL BUSINESS-PERSON: MENTALLY PSYCHED ...DEFENSES PRIMED...MUSCLES TENSED...NEGOTIATING SKILLS POISED LIKE LASERS AT THIS, HER FIRST ASTOUNDING CHALLENGE OF THE YEAR...

EEEEEY YAAAH!!!

...GETTING IN AND OUT OF THE COFFEE ROOM WITHOUT TOUCHING A DONUT.

I WANT TO HAVE A "BEFORE" PICTURE OF ME LOOKING AS FAT AS POSSIBLE IN A LEOTARD FOR MY DIET DIARY, BUT AM TOO EMBARRASSED TO HAVE SOMEONE TAKE IT.

I FINALLY TAKE IT MYSELF IN A MIRROR, BUT AM TOO EMBARRASSED TO GET THE FILM DEVELOPED... I FINALLY GET THE FILM DEVELOPED, BUT AM TOO EMBARRASSED TO PICK IT UP...

AS A PHOTO LAB FULL OF STRANGERS STARE AT MY "FAT PICTURES," I SLOWLY ACCEPT THE ONE HIDEOUS CHOICE I HAVE....

...WHY CAN'T SHE JUST BEG ME TO RETURN THINGS LIKE OTHER DAUGHTERS?

ONE HOUR PHOTO

MY FIRST AEROBICS CLASS IN TEN MONTHS...BUT IT'S OKAY. I'M OKAY. I'M FINE.

I'M HERE. I'M NOT THAT BAD. I'M NOT AS BAD AS I THOUGHT. I'M FINE. I'LL BE FINE. NO SWEAT. I....

AEROBICS

HI. I'M TEENA. I'LL BE YOUR INSTRUCTOR TODAY.

WAAAH!!

IF INADEQUATE PHYSICAL WARM-UP DOESN'T CRIPPLE YOU, INADEQUATE MENTAL WARM-UP WILL.

THE PRE-PACKAGED DESSERT SNACK: ARTIFICIAL FLAVOR... FAKE COLOR... 17 CHEMICALS...

THE GOURMET COOKIE: PURE FRESH CREAM... IMPORTED CHOCOLATE... HAND-GROUND ORGANIC FLOUR... FRESH WHOLE SWEET BUTTER....

FOR THE 1987 DIETER, ANOTHER IMPOSSIBLE QUESTION:

WILL THE FAT STAY WITH ME LONGER IF IT'S MADE OF PRESERVATIVES OR IF IT'S MADE OF QUALITY INGREDIENTS?

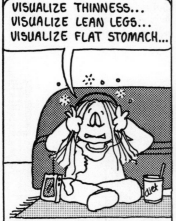

VISUALIZE THINNESS... VISUALIZE LEAN LEGS... VISUALIZE FLAT STOMACH...

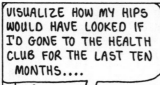

VISUALIZE HOW MY HIPS WOULD HAVE LOOKED IF I'D GONE TO THE HEALTH CLUB FOR THE LAST TEN MONTHS....

DO YOU REALLY THINK THAT DOES ANY GOOD, CATHY?

IT'S 25 SECONDS WHEN I HAVEN'T EATEN ANYTHING.

SUGAR?

OH, NO. I USE ONLY ARTIFICIAL SWEETENER NOW.

I USE ARTIFICIAL SWEETENER AND SO AM ALLOWED ONE TINY CORNER OF A BLUEBERRY MUFFIN...

...A TASTE OF CROISSANT... A SPEC OF LEFTOVER FRUITCAKE... A BITE OF TURNOVER... A TOUCH OF DANISH...

AN OUNCE OF PREVENTION IS WORTH A POUND OF CELLULITE.

YOUR HEALTH CLUB MEMBERSHIP RENEWAL FEE IS $355.00.

$355.00 JUST TO RENEW?!

IT ONLY SEEMS LIKE A LOT WHEN YOU HEAR IT IN ONE LUMP SUM.

AMORTIZED OVER THE GRUELING FITNESS REGIMEN YOU ADHERED TO LAST YEAR, THE FEE WOULD COME TO A MERE...

...$177.50 PER VISIT.

LET'S SEE... YOUR LAST ACTUAL WORKOUT HERE WAS...

AACK! DON'T SAY IT! I DON'T WANT TO HEAR IT!!

AT THAT TIME YOUR WEIGHT WAS...

AACK! DON'T LOOK! DON'T READ IT! DON'T SPEAK IT!!

AND YOU CURRENTLY ARE...

AACK!! DON'T COME NEAR ME WITH THAT TAPE MEASURE!!!

HOW QUICKLY THEY GO FROM A JOG OF MEMORY TO A 10K RUN FROM THE TRUTH.

A PERSON'S WEIGHT IS NO LONGER THE MEASURE OF DIET SUCCESS.

RIGHT... REMOVE SHOES... REMOVE LEG WARMERS...

WHAT COUNTS IS MUSCLE RATIO! CARDIOVASCULAR CAPACITY! OVERALL FITNESS!

RIGHT... REMOVE WATCH... REMOVE EARRINGS...

REMOVE BARRETTES...REMOVE TIGHTS...REMOVE NECKLACE ...REMOVE NAIL POLISH....

IN 1987, THE NUMBERS ON THE SCALE MEAN SOMETHING ENTIRELY DIFFERENT!

MY CONTACT LENSES WEIGH THREE POUNDS EACH!

"SUDDENLY AWARE THAT TIME AND MEN ARE DISAPPEARING, MANY SINGLE WOMEN ARE CLINGING TO RELATIONSHIPS THEY ALREADY HAVE, WITH A NEW FERVOR TO MAKE THEM WORK."

"OTHER WOMEN ARE RESPONDING BY MAKING ONE LAST LEAP INTO THE SINGLES SCENE, FRANTICALLY TRYING TO HANG ONTO YOUTH AND/OR GRAB SOMEONE BETTER."

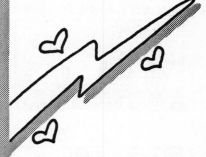

"FROM THESE TWO EXTREMES COMES STILL A THIRD: THAT RARE BUT PROUD PRODUCT OF THE '80s... THE WOMAN WHO DOES IT ALL."

MARRY ME, IRVING! AACK! NO. WAIT. I'M NOT READY. WHERE ARE ALL THE MEN? I HAVE TO MEET NEW MEN NO. WAIT. AACK. ICK. IRVING, COME BACK. WAIT, NO. WHERE'S THE PARTY? AACK!

WHERE'S MY CAMERA?

THIS TIME MANAGEMENT SYSTEM FEATURES DAILY, WEEKLY AND MONTHLY CALENDARS, QUARTERLY PROJECTION GRAPHS AND A BUSINESS CARD FILE.

VERY NICE.

ORGANIZERS

THIS ONE FEATURES SECTIONS FOR FINANCES, STOCK TRACKING, NETWORKING AND GOAL PLANNING, EXPANDABLE TO A 200-CATEGORY DATA BANK.

VERY NICE.

THIS ONE JUST HAS A PLACE TO RECORD YOUR INSECURITIES THAT YOU SPENT ALL YOUR MONEY ON THE WRONG SYSTEM.

SOLD!!

THEY MAY BE SHOPPING FROM THE INTELLECT, BUT THEY'RE STILL BUYING FROM THE HEART.

ORGANIZERS

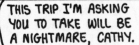

INSIGNIFICANT APPOINTMENTS GET WRITTEN DOWN ON MY HUGE WALL CALENDAR AND CROSS-REFERENCED OVER TO MY NOTE PAD, MEMO REGISTER AND ACTIVITY LOG.

JAN

MEMO

MORE CRITICAL EVENTS GET WRITTEN IN A MORE PRIVATE DESKTOP CALENDAR.... VERY SPECIAL DATES GET WRITTEN IN A TEENSY BOOK IN A SECRET CODE THAT NO ONE CAN READ AND I MAY NEVER REMEMBER.

CALENDAR '87

THE MOST SPECIAL MOMENTS OF ALL ARE NEVER WRITTEN DOWN IN ANY WAY, JUST TOSSED INTO MY MEMORY.

CALENDAR '87

THE MORE IMPORTANT SOMETHING IS TO ME, THE BETTER SYSTEM I HAVE OF MAKING SURE I'LL FORGET IT.

THIS TRIP I'M ASKING YOU TO TAKE WILL BE A NIGHTMARE, CATHY.

PINKLEY

HYSTERICAL, IRATE CLIENT... PICKY, IDIOTIC MEETINGS... COMATOSE DINNERS...

ONLY A REAL PROFESSIONAL WOULD BE ABLE TO SEE PAST THE SURFACE AND APPRECIATE THE DEEPER BENEFITS OF BREAKING YOUR NECK TO MAKE A HIDEOUS TRIP LIKE THIS.

FLIGHT SEGMENTS!!

MY PROTÉGÉE!!

THIS IS A DIRECTORY OF SHOPS AND THEATERS IN THE AREA.

THANK YOU, BUT I'M JUST IN TOWN TO WORK.

THE HOTEL HAS SEVERAL FINE RESTAURANTS, BARS, AND A FULL GYM.

THANKS, BUT I'LL JUST BE STAYING IN MY ROOM TO WORK.

I MUST HAVE NO DISTRACTIONS...NO CALLS...NO NOISE. JUST PURE, SOLID WORK TIME!

LET US KNOW IF YOU NEED ANYTHING.

MY TELEVISION IS BROKEN !!!

TRAVEL IRON... WRINKLE STEAMER... HAIR DRYER... HOT ROLLERS... NAIL DRYER ...MINI-COFFEE MAKER....

CONTACT LENS STERILIZER... ELECTRIC TOOTHBRUSH...TAPE PLAYER... CLOCK RADIO... CALCULATOR...TYPEWRITER...

...AND NOW AN OVERWHELM-ING URGE TO CALL HOME AND SEE IF I'VE GOTTEN ANY MESSAGES.

I DON'T KNOW IF I REALLY CARE ABOUT THE MESSAGES, OR I JUST NEED TO TOUCH BASE WITH THE ONE MACHINE I DIDN'T BRING WITH ME.

THIS IS ROOM 922. I MUST HAVE A 6:30 WAKE-UP CALL.

FINE.

PLEASE DON'T PUT MY WAKE-UP CALL ON THE COMPUTER. IT'S CRITICAL THAT I'M UP AT 6:30 AND I DON'T TRUST THE COMPUTER.

6:30. ROOM 922.

I MUST HAVE YOUR WORD THAT A COMPUT-ER WILL NOT LOSE MY WAKE-UP CALL!!

A COMPUT-ER WILL NOT LOSE YOUR WAKE-UP CALL.

THAT'S WHAT WE HAVE OUR PEOPLE FOR.

"RIP RIP RIP RIP RIP

HOTEL OPERATOR

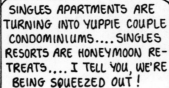

SINGLE-NESS IS DEAD, CATHY.

YOU'RE JUST DEPRESSED BECAUSE IT'S VALENTINE'S WEEK, CHARLENE.

SINGLES APARTMENTS ARE TURNING INTO YUPPIE COUPLE CONDOMINIUMS....SINGLES RESORTS ARE HONEYMOON RETREATS.... I TELL YOU, WE'RE BEING SQUEEZED OUT!

THAT'S NOT TRUE. THERE ARE STILL MILLIONS OF SINGLE PEOPLE OUT HERE LOOKING FOR SOMEONE AFTER WORK.

WHERE'S MY MOM??   CHECK!   THEY'RE JUST SHORTER.

SUSHI BAR -AND- DAY CARE CENTER

HERE'S A GREAT JOKE CARD FOR IRVING, CATHY.

THAT'S WHY YOU AND I ARE STILL SINGLE, CHARLENE. TOO MANY JOKES.

IT'S TIME FOR US TO TAKE A ROMANTIC STAND. TIME TO LAY OUR HEARTS ON THE LINE....

...WHILE KEEPING A SENSE OF COYNESS, OF COURSE. ROMANTIC, BUT NOT TOO INTENSE. SERIOUS, BUT FLIRTATIOUS. LIGHT. YES. COY AND LIGHT.

HERE'S A GREAT JOKE CARD FOR IRVING.

PERFECT.

VALENTINES   VALEN   VALEN   VALENTINES

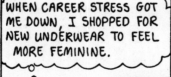

WHEN CAREER STRESS GOT ME DOWN, I SHOPPED FOR NEW UNDERWEAR TO FEEL MORE FEMININE.

Lace an

WHEN I LOST TWO POUNDS, I SHOPPED FOR NEW UNDERWEAR... WHEN I FACED FINANCIAL RUIN, I SHOPPED FOR NEW UNDERWEAR...

NOW I'M TRYING TO REKINDLE A ROMANCE THAT I CAREFULLY BUILT ON INTELLECT AND ENLIGHTENMENT. I'M SHOPPING FOR NEW UNDERWEAR.

WE TRAVEL DOWN SO MANY ROADS IN LIFE, BUT SOMEHOW THEY ALL DUMP OUT IN THE LINGERIE DEPARTMENT.

I BOUGHT SULTRY LINGERIE, BUT I'M TOO EMBARRASSED TO WEAR IT.

I BOUGHT A SUGGESTIVE CARD, BUT I'M TOO EMBARRASSED TO SEND IT.... I BOUGHT A PROVOCATIVE GIFT. I'M TOO EMBARRASSED TO GIVE IT.

I THOUGHT OF RENTING A SEXY MOVIE, BUT I'M TOO EMBARRASSED TO GO PICK ONE OUT AND EVEN IF I DID, I'D BE TOO EMBARRASSED TO ADMIT I HAD IT.

I'M BEGINNING TO UNDERSTAND WHY RED IS THE COLOR OF VALENTINE'S DAY.

CANDY, FLOWERS AND A BRACELET FROM IRVING?? WHAT HAPPENED?! WHAT WENT ON??!

OH, IT'S NOTHING SPECIAL, MOM.

WHAT DOES IT MEAN?? WHAT DID HE SAY?? WHAT DID YOU SAY??

IT'S NOTHING, MOM. REALLY.

I GET TO KNOW THAT YOU GOT ALL THIS, BUT I DON'T GET TO KNOW ANYTHING THAT LED UP TO IT??!

I HAVE TO RUN, NOW.

BEING A MOTHER IS LIKE ONLY GETTING TO READ THE LAST PAGE OF A BOOK.

WE COMPLAIN THAT OUR RELATIONSHIPS GO NOWHERE, BUT DO WE TAKE ANY REAL RESPONSIBILITY? NO.

NO.

NO.

MOST WOMEN CALL ONLY AFTER IT'S SAFE... INITIATE ONLY WHEN WE'RE SURE WE'RE WELCOME.

WE ATTACK MEN FOR LACK OF COMMITMENT, YET EVERY REAL EMOTIONAL RISK IS STILL UP TO THE MAN.... ANY TIME THERE'S A CHANCE FOR GENUINE HUMILIATION, IT'S THE "MAN'S MOVE"!!

I SEE NO NEED TO CHANGE THAT.

ME EITHER.

WHAT'S FOR LUNCH?

82

SURE I CAN'T HELP YOU CARRY THAT IN, CATHY?

YES, IRVING. I'VE WORKED HARD TO EARN MY PROFESSIONAL CREDIBILITY AND DON'T WANT IT TARNISHED BY MORE GOSSIP.

THE PEOPLE IN THIS OFFICE HAVE **ENOUGH** TO TALK ABOUT WITHOUT SEEING YOU WALK IN WITH ME AT 8:00 IN THE MORNING!!

HOW DID HE LIKE THE SEQUINED STOCKINGS?!

SEE WHAT I MEAN?

HOW DO I REKINDLE A ROMANCE WITH SOMEONE I'VE BEEN GOING OUT WITH FOR YEARS, CHARLENE?

I COULD BUY NEW CLOTHES, BUT HE WOULDN'T NOTICE... NEW MAKEUP, HE WOULDN'T CARE... NEW PERFUME, HE WOULDN'T LIKE IT... CHAMPAGNE AND FLOWERS, HE WOULDN'T BE AFFECTED...

SOMETIMES THE ONLY WAY TO RECAPTURE A MAN'S INTEREST IS TO IGNORE HIM FOR A WHILE, CATHY.

IGNORE HIM?? OH, I COULDN'T DO THAT.

THERE'D BE NOTHING TO SHOP FOR!!

DID YOU HAVE A GOOD LUNCH?

FANTASTIC! I DID A 40-MINUTE WORKOUT AND A 3-MILE SWIM!

I DICTATED ALL MY CORRESPONDENCE IN THE JACUZZI!

I STUDIED MY FRENCH LANGUAGE TAPES ON THE STATIONARY CYCLE!

I HIT MY HEART RATE TARGET ZONE AND ENDORPHINE PEAK WHILE MEETING WITH MY BROKER ON SIDE-BY-SIDE ROWING MACHINES!

WHATEVER HAPPENED TO THE GOOD OLD DAYS WHEN "HAVING A GOOD LUNCH" MEANT YOU GOT TO EAT SOMETHING?

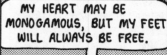

CATHY'S COMING OVER TO DISCUSS IRVING AND I WANT TO BE PREPARED WITH ONE OF THOSE CLASSIC MOTHERLY ONE-LINERS.

A CLASSIC MOTHERLY ONE-LINER?

YOU KNOW, ONE OF THOSE GREAT POIGNANT ONE-LINERS THAT A MOTHER SAYS AND A DAUGHTER REMEMBERS ALL HER LIFE.

I ASKED IRVING TO LIVE WITH ME, MOM.

AAACK!!

THE CLASSIC MOTHERLY ONE-WORDER.

WHAT HAPPENED? WHERE AM I?

CATHY TOLD YOU SHE ASKED IRVING TO LIVE WITH HER AND YOU PASSED OUT.

SHE WHAT? I WHAT??

HAH! AFTER ALL YOUR SELF-RIGHTEOUS SPEECHES ABOUT LETTING HER LIVE HER OWN LIFE, YOU TOTALLY SHORT-CIRCUITED!

I WAS JUST KIDDING. IT'S FINE WITH ME IF THEY LIVE TOGETHER.

AACK!

WE MAY HAVE LOST CONTROL OF OUR OFFSPRING, BUT WE STILL HAVE EACH OTHER....

EVER SINCE ANDREA AND LUKE GOT MARRIED I'VE DREAMED THAT ONE DAY YOU AND I WOULD SURPRISE THEM WITH THE NEWS THAT WE WERE GOING TO TRY LIVING TOGETHER, IRVING...

JUST IMAGINE...WE COULD ACTUALLY TURN INTO THE KIND OF SANE COUPLE THAT THEY ARE.

I'VE THOUGHT OF A MILLION WAYS TO TELL THEM AND NOW THAT WE'RE HERE....

DING DONG!

WHAT??!

...WORDS ESCAPE ME.

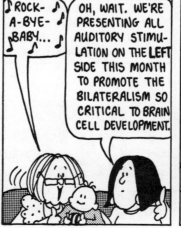

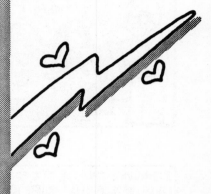

I'LL TAKE ZENITH SO YOU TWO CAN TALK.

OK. REMEMBER OUR RESPONSE SEQUENCE FOR FUSSING, HONEY.

WAAH!

1. PLAY THE DVOŘÁK PIANO QUINTET IN "A"...
2. 2-MINUTE SILENT ROCK WITH HEAD PAT...
3. 4-MINUTE "BOUNCY WALK" TO INDIAN HARVEST CHANT..
4. ITALIAN LULLABYE...

WAAH!

NOTHING COMFORTS AN IN- FANT LIKE HAVING ALL PRI- MARY CARE-GIVERS FOLLOW THE SAME FAMILIAR PATTERNS OF SOUND AND TOUCH!

QUIT CRYING AND I'LL GIVE YOU A CAR.

DA!

I THOUGHT YOU WOULD HAVE FOUND ANOTHER JOB AND GONE BACK TO WORK BY NOW, ANDREA.

IT'S SO HARD TO KNOW WHAT TO DO, CATHY...

I MEAN, I THINK I KNOW WHAT'S RIGHT AND THEN I THINK ABOUT THE ENDLESS MEANINGLESS CHORES...

THE HASSLES...THE LOSS OF CONTROL.....DO THE REWARDS REALLY JUSTIFY HAVING EVERY SECOND OF THE DAY DICTATED BY THE MIND OF AN INFANT??

IS THAT A DE- SCRIPTION OF BEING A MOTHER OR HAVING A CAREER?

LIKE I SAID, IT GETS CON- FUSING...

YOU LAUGHED AT HOW I USED TO PAT MY STOMACH AND COACH ZENITH'S LEG KICKS BEFORE SHE WAS BORN, ...BUT VOILÁ! SHE WAS CRAWLING AT FIVE MONTHS!!

WHAT WAS THE BIG RUSH?

OH, CATHY, IT'S HER FIRST HUGE HURDLE OVER FEELING HELP- LESS IN LIFE! I COULDN'T WAIT FOR HER TO KNOW SHE HAS ANOTHER CHOICE!

ONCE A WOMAN HAS EXPERI- ENCED THE THRILL OF MOVING FORWARD BY HER OWN POWER, A WHOLE WORLD OF KNOWLEDGE OPENS UP TO HER!!

YEEHAAA

...TODAY WE'RE GOING TO LEARN ABOUT SIT- TING STILL, HONEY.....

IRVING AGREED TO LIVE WITH YOU... THEN RAN SCREAMING FROM LUKE AND ANDREA'S HOUSE...AND YOU HAVEN'T HEARD FROM HIM SINCE??

OH, HE JUST NEEDS TIME TO ADJUST.

THAT'S THE GREAT THING ABOUT MEN OUR AGE... THEY'RE REALLY MELLOWING INTO VERY REASONABLE, PREDICTABLE PEOPLE.

IRVING MAY HAVE RUN OFF A LUNATIC, BUT I KNOW THE NEXT TIME HE WALKS THROUGH THIS DOOR, HE'LL BE..

...A JUNGLE SAFARI GUIDE.

IRVING, WHAT ARE YOU DOING IN DUCK HUNTING BOOTS??

I'VE ALWAYS BEEN FASCINATED WITH DUCK HUNTING.

YOU'VE NEVER EVEN HELD A FLY SWATTER BEFORE.

THIS HAPPENS TO BE MY OUTBACK GEAR.

OUTBACK? WHAT WOULD YOU DO IN THE OUTBACK?

CATHY, THIS IS 1987! GET WITH THE PROGRAM! I'M GOING TO DO WHAT EVERYONE IS DOING!!!

...I'M GOING TO GO SIT IN THE JUNGLE AND WAIT FOR MY HAIR TO GROW OUT.

IRVING, WHAT'S HAPPENED TO YOU??

MEN HAVE HAD IT WITH WIMP CLOTHES, CATHY.

LOOK AT THIS STUFF...EXPEDITION CANVAS PANTS TOUGH ENOUGH TO SURVIVE A ROCK SLIDE...VESTS THAT CAN LUG 100 POUNDS OF GEAR WHILE BLOCKING GALE-FORCE WINDS...FATIGUE SOCKS... STORM FLAPS...GROMMET VENTS...TRAMPING BOOTS...

THIS HAT ALONE CAN WITHSTAND EVERYTHING FROM THE SCORCHING HEAT OF THE AMAZON TO THE FRIGID BLASTS OF THE ANTARCTIC.

OH, FORGET IT. LET'S JUST GO GET SOMETHING TO EAT.

IT'S DRIZZLING OUT.

32 POCKETS IN YOUR VEST...
21 POCKETS IN YOUR SHIRT...
15 POCKETS IN YOUR PANTS...
3 POCKETS IN YOUR BELT...
7 POCKETS IN YOUR BOOTS...

I'M STARTING TO LIKE IT, IRVING.

YOU ARE ??

YOU LOOK LIKE A GIANT PURSE.

THE SHOCK OF REALIZING YOUR SINGLE DAYS WOULD BE OVER IF WE MOVED IN TOGETHER WAS SO BIG THAT YOU RAN OUT AND GOT A WHOLE NEW HAIRDO AND WARDROBE.

WHAT DID YOU THINK? THAT IF YOU CHANGED THE WAY YOU LOOKED THE FUTURE MIGHT NOT RECOGNIZE YOU?? THAT IT WOULD LET YOU JUST SLIDE BY WITHOUT GROWING UP??

I CAN'T BELIEVE IT.

HOW CAN MEN BE SO JUVENILE ??

WHERE'S IRVING?

HE TOOK HIS PARATROOPER BAG AND WENT OFF TO HUNT DOWN SOME COFFEE FILTERS IN HIS NEW 4-WHEEL-DRIVE VEHICLE.

HE'S SNAPPED, HUH?

LET'S JUST SAY HE'S HAD A SLIGHT OVERREACTION TO THE IDEA OF LIVING TOGETHER.

WELL, IT'S NORMAL. I MEAN, SAY ALL YOU WANT ABOUT OUR SIMILARITIES, THERE'S ONE KEY DIFFERENCE BETWEEN MEN AND WOMEN THAT WILL NEVER CHANGE...

YEAH...

WHEN MEN RUN FROM A RELATIONSHIP, THEY'RE COWARDS..... WHEN WE RUN, WE'RE TAKING TIME TO GAIN INSIGHT AND PERSPECTIVE!!

WHERE'S MY TAX FORM? WHERE'S THE FILE THAT'S SUPPOSED TO HOLD MY W-2 FORM AND INTEREST STATEMENT?

WHERE'S THE MILEAGE LOG I SPECIFICALLY ASKED BE KEPT LAST YEAR?? WHERE'S THE MONTHLY CHECK SUMMARY?

AND WHO'S BEEN STUFFING VISA RECEIPTS IN THE ALUMINUM FOIL DRAWER ??!!

BAM BAM

HOW EMBARRASSING. I'M SURROUNDED BY IDIOTS AND I'M THE ONLY ONE IN THE OFFICE.

EXHAUSTED, DEHYDRATED, THE BODY SCREAMS FOR WATER.

NAH... I THINK I'LL HAVE A CHERRY COLA.

Aerobics Class

REFRESHMEN

NERVES FRAZZLED, BRAIN FRAYED, THE BODY BEGS FOR PURE, NATURAL VITAMINS.

NAH... I FEEL LIKE A DOVE BAR.

A TEENSY BIT DROWSY AT THE THOUGHT OF DOING TAXES, THE EYELIDS DROOP ONCE.

YES! SLEEP!! I MUST NEED SLEEP! IF I'M THIS TIRED AT 8 P.M., I NEED SLEEP!!

INCOME TAX INFO.

THE ONLY TIME I EVER LISTEN TO MY BODY IS WHEN IT TELLS ME TO DO SOMETHING I'LL REGRET.

I HAVE TO BUY A BOOK! I HAVE TO BUY A BOOK! I CAN'T POSSIBLY DO MY TAXES UNTIL I BUY A BOOK!!

CATHY, EVERY TIME PEOPLE CAN'T COPE WITH SOMETHING THEY BUY A BOOK. MILLIONS OF PEOPLE SPEND MILLIONS ON BOOKS EACH YEAR JUST TO PROCRASTINATE.

YOU DO NOT HAVE TO BUY A BOOK!

YOU'RE RIGHT.

I HAVE TO WRITE A BOOK!!

94

IT MAKES ME SICK TO THINK THE MONEY I WORKED SO HARD FOR COULD BE USED TO BUY MORE GUNS FOR THE CONTRAS.

LET'S SEE ...NOPE. WE DON'T HAVE YOU DOWN FOR CONTRA AID.

IRS INFO.

AND I DO **NOT** WANT MY TAX MONEY USED FOR NUCLEAR PLANNING OF ANY KIND. NO WEAPONS. NO TESTING.

NOPE. NO NUKES.

YOUR ENTIRE TAX PAYMENT FOR 1986 WILL BE USED TO BUY REFRESHMENTS FOR THE SPECIAL SQUAD INVESTIGATING THE $10,000 OUR VICE PRESIDENT SPENDS EACH YEAR GIVING OUT PLAYING CARDS ON AIR FORCE TWO.

AAAGH!!

DON'T FEEL BAD. LAST YEAR YOU POPPED FOR THE CARDS.

IRS INFO.

ARE YOUR TAXES REALLY AS COMPLICATED AS ALL THIS, MOM??

THIS? OH, THIS IS NOTHING!

YOUR GRANDMOTHER COULD TURN A COUPLE OF SALES SLIPS INTO A CARTON OF CLIPPINGS!

GRANDPA COULD PARLAY ONE INTEREST STATEMENT INTO A MOUNTAIN OF DOCUMENTATION!

THEIR CANCELED CHECKS ONCE TOOK OVER THE WHOLE GUEST ROOM!!

IT'S JUST A KNACK PEOPLE IN OUR FAMILY HAVE ALWAYS HAD, CATHY.

IF WE CAN'T MAKE MORE OF OUR MONEY, AT LEAST WE MAKE MORE OF OUR MESSES!!

I'M DOOMED.

I WENT THROUGH ALL THE PAPERS AND CLIPPED ARTICLES ON DOING YOUR OWN TAXES, BUT I KNOW YOU DON'T HAVE TIME TO READ THEM, CATHY.

I TAPED FINANCIAL SHOWS, BUT KNOW YOU DON'T HAVE TIME TO WATCH THEM... I TOOK THE AUDIO TRACK OFF THE VIDEO, BUT YOU WON'T HAVE TIME TO LISTEN TO IT.

I TOOK NOTES, BUT YOU WON'T HAVE TIME TO REVIEW THEM. SO, ANYWAY, I JUST WANTED TO LET YOU KNOW I WON'T BE BOTHERING YOU WITH ANY OF THIS.

WAAH!!

GOOD THING I STOPPED BY. YOU SEEM A LITTLE DEPRESSED.

YES, I KNOW THAT IF I'D STARTED IT A YEAR AGO, THE BENEFITS WOULD HAVE BEEN COMPOUNDING DAILY, AND THAT BY WAITING UNTIL THE LAST SECOND I'M ONLY CHEATING MYSELF.

I KNOW THAT EVEN THOUGH IT'S A PAIN TO DO IN THE SHORT TERM, THAT WHEN I'M OLD AND GRAY, IT COULD MAKE A HUGE DIFFERENCE IN THE QUALITY OF MY LIFE.

I PLANNED TO DO IT BEFORE. I PLAN TO DO IT IN THE FUTURE. I JUST DIDN'T DO IT YET, OK ??!!

IRAs: THE DENTAL FLOSS OF THE BANKING INDUSTRY.

MY ASSETS? AH, YES. I'VE INVESTED ALL MY ASSETS IN THE WOMEN'S SHOE INDUSTRY.

HEE, HEE. I INVESTED MINE IN THE DIET SODA INDUSTRY.

I PUT ALL MY MONEY IN THE GROWTH INDUSTRY OF FOAMING HAIR PRODUCTS!

HA, HA! YES! EXCEPT FOR THE FUNDS WE DIVERTED INTO THE CHOCOLATE CHIP COOKIE INDUSTRY!!!

HA, HA! I DUMPED MY WHOLE BONUS IN THE WRINKLE CREME INDUSTRY!!

I DROPPED $300 ALONE IN TEXTURED HOSE!!

HOO, HA! $2,000 IN THE PHONE COMPANY!!

AT LEAST YOU STILL HAVE YOUR SENSE OF HUMOR.

IT'S THE ONE THING WE COULDN'T SPEND.

ATTENTION ALL EMPLOYEES: I KNOW THAT WORKING HERE HAS DESTROYED YOUR HEALTH, RUINED YOUR RELATIONSHIPS, AND WADDED YOUR CAREER ENTHUSIASM INTO LITTLE PILES OF TRASH.

YOU'VE EARNED JUST ENOUGH TO DIG YOURSELVES INTO HOPELESS FINANCIAL CAVERNS AND TODAY, APRIL 15, YOU'VE TOTALLY BOTTOMED OUT. I JUST WANT YOU TO KNOW THAT EVEN THOUGH I DON'T PAY ANY INCOME TAX MYSELF, I UNDERSTAND. I CARE. I'M HERE FOR YOU!

SPLAT!

IT WAS WORTH A SHOT.

RUN FOR YOUR LIFE.

IF THE ONLY WAY I CAN DO BETTER ON MY TAXES NEXT YEAR IS TO BUY A HOUSE, THEN FINE, I'LL LOOK AT HOUSES.

YOU CAN'T, CATHY! WHAT ABOUT IRVING?

I'M SICK OF PUTTING OFF MY WHOLE LIFE WHILE I WAIT FOR SOME GUY, CHARLENE. I DON'T HAVE ANY REAL FURNITURE YET BECAUSE I'VE BEEN WAITING FOR SOME GUY... I HAVE NO DISHES BECAUSE I'VE BEEN WAITING FOR SOME GUY...

I HAVE NO GOOD STEREO EQUIP-MENT...NO GOOD PANS...NO NICE TOWELS...NO DE-CENT LAMPS... NO ART...ZILCH. ZILCH. ZILCH!

YEAH... IT'S A QUESTION EVERY WOMAN COMES TO SOONER OR LATER...

IF I HAVEN'T BOUGHT ANYTHING YET, WHY DON'T I HAVE ANY MONEY ??

YOU'RE REALLY GOING TO BUY A HOUSE, CATHY?

YES I AM, CHAR-LENE, AND I'M TAKING MY DAD OUT TO LUNCH TO CELEBRATE MY DECISION!

YOUR DAD?

I GUESS IN A WAY I'VE FOLLOWED MORE IN HIS FOOTSTEPS.

I DON'T THINK ANYONE BUT A FATHER WOULD UNDER-STAND WHAT A MOMENT LIKE THIS MEANS !!

HOW MUCH?

$75,000.00

OF COURSE THE PROBLEM WITH A WOMAN BUYING HER OWN HOUSE IS THAT SHE NO LONGER LOOKS MOVE-IN-ABLE, CATHY.

"MOVE-IN-ABLE"?

YES. A WOMAN SHOULD OWN ENOUGH ON HER OWN TO DEM-ONSTRATE HER TASTE LEVEL AND COPING ABILITY, BUT NEVER SO MUCH THAT SHE DOESN'T LOOK MOVE-IN-ABLE.

I'M SUPPOSED TO BE THIN, GORGEOUS, TONED, TAN, WRINKLE-FREE, SEXY, SUC-CESSFUL, AND NOW I'M ALSO SUPPOSED TO LOOK "MOVE-IN-ABLE" ??!!

LET'S JUST SAY YOU SHOULD FIT IN A U-HAUL.

LET'S JUST SAY I'M HOLDING OUT FOR A MOVING VAN.

WELL, HOORAY FOR OUR SECRETARIES. ANYTHING TO ADD, CHARLENE?

YES.

SECRETARIES WEEK

98.5% OF THE SECRETARIES IN THE COUNTRY ARE WOMEN, AND YET THE MEASLY 1.5% WHO ARE MEN MAKE 33% MORE A YEAR THAN WE DO!! WHILE WE SALUTE SECRETARIES THIS WEEK, LET'S ALSO TURN OUR ATTENTION TO THE POLICY-MAKERS WHO HAVE MADE ATROCITIES LIKE THIS A REALITY!!

ANYONE CAN MAKE A TOAST, BUT IT TAKES A WOMAN TO REALLY GET A PARTY GOING.

SECRETARIES WEEK

AS YOUR SECRETARY-RECEPTIONIST, I'M THE FIRST PERSON HERE IN THE MORNING AND THE LAST PERSON TO GO HOME, MR. PINKLEY.

SECRETARIES WEEK

I RUN... I SLAVE... I SHARE EVERY DISASTER...I KNOW MORE ABOUT WHAT GOES ON IN THIS COMPANY THAN ANYONE AND YET I MAKE LESS MONEY THAN THE LOWEST FLUNKY ON THE TOTEM POLE!!

AH, BUT I'M THE ONE WHO CAN'T SLEEP AT NIGHT, CHARLENE.

NO WONDER YOU CAN'T SLEEP AT NIGHT!!

SECRETARIES WEEK

LET'S SEE...PUT, "HAVE A HAPPY SECRETARIES DAY."

..NO, WAIT...MAKE IT, "HAVE A MARVELOUS SECRETARIES DAY".. ..NO, WAIT..."HAVE A GREAT SECRETARIES DAY"....

...NO, WAIT...WAIT...MAKE IT, "HAVE A WONDERFUL SECRETARIES DAY"... NO, WAIT... "..A SUPER.." NO..WAIT....

Have the Secretaries Day you've always dreamed of.

THE EXOTIC OUTFIT: NO IMPACT.... THE PHONY INTEREST IN SPORTS: NO IMPACT....

THE LONG MEANINGFUL TALKS: NO IMPACT.... THE SILENT TREATMENT: NO IMPACT....

THE $5,000 OF NEW MAKE-UP, PERFUME, JEWELRY AND SELF-HELP MANUALS: NO IMPACT....

THE PROPERLY TIMED PIECE OF STALE PIZZA:

IMPACT.

OH, YOU DOLL! PERFECT! I LOVE YOU!!

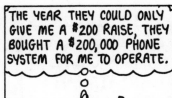
 WHEN I STARTED HERE AT $10,000 A YEAR, THEY GOT ME A $3,000 TYPEWRITER TO TYPE ON.

 THE YEAR THEY COULD ONLY GIVE ME A $200 RAISE, THEY BOUGHT A $200,000 PHONE SYSTEM FOR ME TO OPERATE.

 THE YEAR I GOT A $300 RAISE, THEY BOUGHT AN $11,000 COPIER, A $4,000 FAX MACHINE AND A $1,500,000 COMPUTER SYSTEM FOR ME TO USE.

 WHY DO I GET THE FEELING I'D BE MORE VALUABLE TO THIS COMPANY IF I CAME WITH A PLUG?

 WHAT DID MR. PINKLEY GIVE YOU FOR SECRETARIES WEEK, CHARLENE?

SECRETARIES WEEK

 I TOLD HIM NOT TO BOTHER.

YOU TOLD HIM NOT TO BOTHER??

 OH, CATHY, WHEN A SECRETARY KNOWS SOMEONE AS WELL AS I KNOW MR. PINKLEY, SHE DOESN'T NEED HIM TO RUN OUT AND BUY LITTLE TRINKETS!

 ...SHE CAN PHONE IN HER GIFT ORDER AND CHARGE IT TO HIS AMERICAN EXPRESS NUMBER.

SECRETARIES WEEK

 IF YOU DON'T LIKE SECRETARIAL PAY, WHY DON'T YOU GET A BETTER JOB, CHARLENE?

ONCE YOU'VE BEEN LABELED AS A SECRETARY, IT'S IMPOSSIBLE TO RISE ABOVE IT WITHOUT GOING TO ANOTHER COMPANY AND LYING ABOUT YOUR PAST.

 PLUS, EVEN IN TWO-CAREER HOMES, WOMEN STILL DO 75% OF THE HOUSEWORK AND CHILD CARE, SAPPING US OF BOTH THE TIME AND ENERGY MEN HAVE TO BETTER THEIR LOTS.

 WHO CAN ADVANCE WHEN EVERY SECOND OF OUR LIVES IS SPENT JUST TRYING TO KEEP UP WITH OTHER PEOPLE'S BUSYWORK?!

SECRETARIES

 GOOD POINT. WHY DON'T YOU RESEARCH THAT ALL OUT, TYPE IT UP AND COLLATE A FEW COPIES FOR MY FILES?

SECRETARIES WEEK

I'M THINKING ABOUT GOING TO A REALTOR AND LOOKING FOR A HOUSE, IRVING.

A HOUSE? GREAT.

REALLY? OF COURSE I'VE DREAMED WE COULD DO THIS TOGETHER, BUT THE SMALLEST MENTION OF COMMITMENT SEEMS TO SEND YOU FARTHER INTO THE JUNGLE.

DON'T BE SILLY.

REALLY?? MAYBE WE COULD JUST DRIVE PAST THE...

NOT TODAY, DARLING. THE HIPPO-POTAMI ARE FEEDING.

TAKE ME.

NO, I'M NOT MARRIED. I'M LOOKING FOR A HOUSE FOR MYSELF.

AH, YES. I UNDERSTAND. YOU GAVE UP.

I GAVE UP??

YOU GAVE UP FINDING A HUSBAND.

I DID NOT "GIVE UP"!

WELL, OF COURSE YOU'LL SAY YOU DIDN'T GIVE UP... BUT SOME TEENSY PART OF YOU IS HERE BECAUSE YOU GAVE UP.

I GIVE UP.

SHE GAVE UP.

SO OFTEN, HAPPINESS IS THE EXTENT TO WHICH WE BALANCE OUR GRANDIOSE EXPECTATIONS WITH REALITY.

NEW LISTINGS

NOWHERE IS THIS AS TRUE AS IN REAL ESTATE, WHERE THE PURCHASE OF YOUR FIRST HOME HITS YOU SMACK IN THE FACE WITH NOT ONLY YOUR LOT IN LIFE, BUT YOUR STREET IN LIFE.

OF COURSE, A WOMAN WHO'S AS SUCCESSFUL AS YOU OBVIOUSLY ARE MUST BE ABLE TO SPEND ABOUT...

THAT'S IT?!!

...SO OFTEN, HAPPINESS IS THE EXTENT TO WHICH WE BALANCE OUR GRANDIOSE EXPECTATIONS WITH REALITY....

"MONDAY: ATE HALF A GRAPEFRUIT BEFORE WORK. WAS SELF-RIGHTEOUS AND EFFICIENT."

"TUESDAY: ATE ONE SLICE OF DRY WHEAT TOAST. WAS PROUD AND POLITE."

"TODAY: ATE FOUR CHOCOLATE DONUTS. WAS SO CHARGED WITH SELF-DISGUST I STORMED INTO PINKLEY'S OFFICE AND DEMANDED A SALARY REVIEW."

ONE WOMAN'S DOWNFALL IS ANOTHER WOMAN'S POWER BREAKFAST.

WHEN I FIRST MET IRVING, YOU SAID, "KEEP IT LIGHT. KEEP IT COOL. MEN HATE TO BE PUSHED."

TWO YEARS INTO THE RELATIONSHIP YOU SAID, "KEEP IT LIGHT, KEEP IT COOL. MEN HATE TO BE PUSHED."

NOW IRVING AND I ARE ACTUALLY DISCUSSING THE POSSIBILITY OF LIVING TOGETHER, AND YOUR ONLY ADVICE IS, "KEEP IT LIGHT. KEEP IT COOL. MEN HATE TO BE PUSHED"??

WHAT'S WRONG WITH THAT?

WHEN DO I GET TO ACT LIKE I LIKE HIM?!

I THINK I'M AFRAID TO ASK FOR A RAISE BECAUSE GETTING ONE PROBABLY MEANS I COULD HAVE GOTTEN ONE BEFORE IF I'D TRIED, IRVING.

IN A WAY, TO SUCCEED TOMORROW MEANS I'VE FAILED TO BE WHAT I COULD HAVE BEEN FOR THE WHOLE LAST YEAR.

THE ONLY WAY TO FEEL GOOD ABOUT THE LAST YEAR IS IF I GET TURNED DOWN FOR A RAISE, IN WHICH CASE I'LL FEEL LIKE A PAST SUCCESS BUT A CURRENT FAILURE.

WHAT DO YOU THINK?

WHY COULDN'T I HAVE BEEN BORN BEFORE MEN WERE SUPPOSED TO BE SUPPORTIVE?

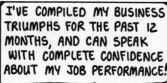

Panel 1: READY TO NEGOTIATE YOUR RAISE, CATHY? / YES. I'M WEARING MY POWER OUTFIT AND HAVE PRACTICED MY AUTHORITATIVE WALK.

Panel 2: I'VE COMPILED MY BUSINESS TRIUMPHS FOR THE PAST 12 MONTHS, AND CAN SPEAK WITH COMPLETE CONFIDENCE ABOUT MY JOB PERFORMANCE!

Panel 3: CAN YOU SAY THE AMOUNT YOU'RE ASKING FOR WITHOUT LAUGHING? / CERTAINLY. I WANT FI...HEE HEE ...FIV HEE HOO HEE....

Panel 4: HEE HOO HA HA HOO!! / HER PRESENTATION'S READY, BUT SHE'S STILL FIXING HER FACE.

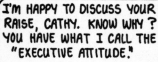

Panel 5: I'M HAPPY TO DISCUSS YOUR RAISE, CATHY. KNOW WHY? YOU HAVE WHAT I CALL THE "EXECUTIVE ATTITUDE."

Panel 6: YOU HAVE A REAL KNOWLEDGE OF THE FINANCIAL STRAIN THIS COMPANY'S BEEN UNDER... YOU HAVE THE VISION TO SEE PAST A QUICK CASH FIX TO THE LONG-TERM REWARDS....

Panel 7: AND YOU HAVE SOMETHING EVEN MORE IMPORTANT... / A LIST OF THE SALARIES OF ALL THE OTHER EMPLOYEES.

Panel 8: AAACK!! / "ACKERLY, $42,000... ABBOTT, $55,000... BAILEY, $61,000...."

Panel 9: $5,000. YES. THAT'S WHAT I ASKED FOR. A $5,000 RAISE. / CATHY...CATHY... YOU FORGET! I KNOW YOU!!

Panel 10: I'VE SEEN YOU CRY ABOUT YOUR BOYFRIEND! I'VE SEEN YOU SNEAK BACK INTO THE CONFERENCE ROOM AND EAT ALL THE DONUTS!...I KNOW YOU'RE NOT THAT TOUGH!!

Panel 11: I SAW YOU AT THE OFFICE CHRISTMAS PARTY, MR. PINKLEY. / WE'LL RECONVENE TOMORROW.

Panel 12: HOW ARE THE BIG NEGOTIATIONS GOING? / I'M DOWN 32 DONUTS, BUT UP ONE DRUNKEN STUPOR.

111

OF COURSE, FOR HARD-TO-FIT SHAPES, THERE'S ALWAYS THE MATURE SUIT RACK.

OH, NO. NOT THE MATURE SUIT RACK!

BUILT-IN PLASTIC CUPS... FULL SKIRTS...

I WILL NOT WEAR A SUIT FROM THE MATURE SUIT RACK!

YOU CAN WEAR A YOUNG SUIT AND HAVE EVERYONE SEE YOUR FIGURE PROBLEMS, OR YOU CAN WEAR A MATURE SUIT AND HAVE EVERYONE GUESS EXACTLY WHAT IT IS YOU'RE TRYING TO HIDE!

GOOD CHOICE. THE TRUTH IS BRUTAL, BUT THE IMAGINATION'S EVEN WORSE.

SORRY, BUT I HAVE TO RUN, MOM.

BYE, CATHY!

BYE!

I THINK SHE WAS TRYING TO SAY THINGS ARE FINE.... DAD, WHAT'S YOUR OPINION ON THAT?

I CONCUR. HOWEVER, I NOTICED A LITTLE TENSION IN HER VOICE.

YES. I INTERPRETED THE TENSION AS LACK OF SLEEP.

AH. POSSIBLE. I MAY HAVE DETECTED A YAWN.

BUT THE HURRY. WHAT DO YOU MAKE OF IT?

YES. LET'S EXPLORE THE HURRIED ASPECT....

IT TAKES AN EXPERIENCED TEAM TO TURN A FIVE SECOND MESSAGE INTO AN EVENING OF COMMENTARY.

IT USED TO BE THAT ALL THE WOMEN I KNEW WERE SINGLE AND THEY WERE ALL FRIENDS.

THEN SOME OF THEM GOT MARRIED. FINE. I STILL HAD MY SINGLE FRIENDS. SOME HAD CHILDREN. FINE. I STILL HAD MY CHILDLESS SINGLE FRIENDS. SOME STARTED WORKING OUT AND PERFECTING THEMSELVES. FINE. JUST FINE.

NOW I'M SEARCHING FOR A SLIGHTLY OVERWEIGHT, SINGLE, CHILDLESS WOMAN WHO DOESN'T HAVE A DATE AND ISN'T TOO DEPRESSING TO BE AROUND.

IT'S GETTING HARDER TO FIND A GIRLFRIEND THAN A BOYFRIEND.

113

THANK YOU, AND MAY I ADD MY PERSONAL WELCOME TO "THE LAST RESORT" HEALTH SPA. IT'S GOOD TO SEE SOME NEW FACES AS WELL AS SOME VERY FAMILIAR ONES.

YOU'VE BEEN GIVEN SCHEDULES AND HAD A TWO-HOUR LECTURE ON PHYSIOLOGY, KINESIOLOGY, DETOXIFICATION AND NUTRITIONAL DYNAMICS.

IT'S A LOT TO ABSORB, BUT IF ANYONE HAS ANY QUESTIONS, I'LL BE HAPPY TO ANSWER.

WHO'S BEEN HERE BEFORE AND HOW FAT WERE THEY THE LAST TIME??!

YEAH!

pant, pant, WHEW!

GREAT! KEEP IT UP!!

THE PRE-DAWN FIVE-MILE HIKE IS A GREAT WAY TO WARM UP THE MUSCLES FOR THE DAY OF EXERCISE AHEAD.

SHOUTING OPENS THE LUNGS AND OXYGENATES THE WHOLE BLOOD SUPPLY... SO LET'S HEAR IT! LET'S MAKE SOME NOISE!!

YEAH!

GO! GO!

TAXI!!

I'M STARVING. I'M IN PAIN.

ONLY TWO MORE HOURS UNTIL SNACK TIME.

I'M EXHAUSTED. I CAN'T GO ON!

ONLY 45 MORE MINUTES UNTIL SNACK TIME.

....YOU MADE IT! SNACK TIME!

POTASSIUM BROTH?? I WORKED FIVE HOURS FOR SIX OUNCES OF POTASSIUM BROTH?

BLEAH!! BLEAH!! BLEAH!!

THERE'S NOTHING SO INSPIRING AS A CLIENT WHO GOES BEYOND THE PRESCRIBED EXERCISES.

AFTER A DAY OF EXERCISE, YOGA HELPS US QUIETLY RE-FLECT ON OUR INNER SELVES... ..PICTURE THE BLOOD FLOWING TO YOUR FINGERTIPS... PICTURE YOUR PEACEFUL BRAIN CELLS...

PICTURE THE PROGRESS YOU'RE MAKING THAT'S MUCH MORE IMPORTANT THAN JUST NUM-BERS ON THE SCALE...

I LOST FOUR INCHES!!

YOGA

PICTURE THAT WE'RE ALL STILL SITTING IN THE YOGA ROOM.

WEIGH-IN ROOM

FOR THE "WAX WRAP" TREATMENT, YOU NEED TO REMOVE YOUR CLOTHES AND HOP IN THIS TUB.

I BEG YOUR PAR-DON?

REMOVE YOUR CLOTHES AND HOP IN THIS TUB. THEN I'LL POUR WARM WAX OVER YOUR ENTIRE BODY AND WRAP YOU IN SARAN WRAP!

YOU WANT ME TO LIE NAKED IN THIS TUB WHILE YOU POUR WAX ON ME AND WRAP ME IN SARAN WRAP??

YES. IT WORKS WON-DERS!

DOES IT DISSOLVE THE FAT OR JUST EMBARRASS IT INTO LEAVING?

THIS IS MY LUNCH??

THAT'S YOUR 300-CALORIE LUNCH.

THIS IS A 300-CALORIE LUNCH??

THAT'S A 300-CALORIE LUNCH.

WHEN I MAKE A 300-CALORIE LUNCH, IT'S 25 TIMES MORE FOOD THAN THIS.

Panel 1: I'M DIETING FOR ME. I WANT TO FEEL GOOD ABOUT ME! — EXCELLENT, BETH!

Panel 2: I'M DIETING BECAUSE MY BODY IS MY TEMPLE AND I RESPECT IT! — EXCELLENT, KIM!

Panel 3: I'M DIETING TO MAKE CHARLENE SICK! TO MAKE ANDREA FEEL FAT! AND SO EVERY MAN I'VE EVER MET WILL HATE HIMSELF FOR HAVING BLOWN HIS BIG CHANCE WITH ME! HA HA!

Panel 4: WE WORK SO MUCH HARDER WHEN WE PUT THE FEELINGS OF OTHERS BEFORE OUR OWN.

Panel 5: TWO POUNDS?? I'VE EXERCISED TEN HOURS A DAY ON 800 CALORIES AND I'VE ONLY LOST TWO POUNDS??! — THE LAST RE... WEIGH-IN ROOM — BAM BAM — STAFF

Panel 6: LOSING WEIGHT IS LIKE WAITING FOR SOMEONE TO RETURN A PHONE CALL, CATHY. — THE LAST RE... WEIGH... ROOM

Panel 7: ONCE YOU'VE PUT OUT THE EFFORT, SOME PEOPLE RESPOND RIGHT AWAY...SOME WAIT A WEEK...BUT SOME WAIT UNTIL YOU'VE GIVEN UP ALL HOPE AND DONE SOMETHING TOTALLY STUPID FOR REVENGE! — STAFF

Panel 8: I KNEW THAT MEN AND FAT WERE RELATED.

Panel 9: I FEEL SO DISCOURAGED. — YOU EXPECTED TO LOSE WEIGHT TOO FAST, CATHY. — THE LAST RESORT Cycle Room

Panel 10: WEIGHT **LOSS** CAN NEVER BE INSTANTANEOUS, JUST AS WEIGHT **GAIN** IS NEVER INSTANTANEOUS. — Cycle Room

Panel 11: DO YOU REALIZE HOW LONG IT TOOK YOUR BODY TO GAIN JUST **FIVE** OF THOSE POUNDS? — TWENTY MINUTES WITH A PACKAGE OF DOVE BARS.

Panel 12: ...OH. WAIT... I DON'T SEE THAT IN HERE... — I'M SURROUNDED BY AMATEURS. — THE LAST R... Cycle Room

119

DEAR MOM...I'M LYING NAKED IN A VAT OF SEAWEED PASTE, BREATHING THROUGH A PLASTIC STRAW AND LISTENING TO A TAPE OF THE MATING CALL OF THE ARCTIC WALRUS.

The Last Resort

IF THE ROOF COLLAPSES AND I'M CRUSHED IN THIS TUB BY FALLING PLASTER, I WANT YOU TO KNOW I WAS NOT FORCED INTO THIS BY ANY ONE PERSON...I CHOSE TO BE HERE, IN A FRANTIC ATTEMPT TO MEET THE BEAUTY STANDARDS EXPECTED OF A WOMAN IN 1987.

The Last Resort Health Spa

SUE THE WORLD.

The Last Resort Health Spa

I'LL GIVE YOU $10 FOR THAT RADISH.

THE RADISH IS NOT FOR SALE.

The Last Resort DINING ROOM

YOU'RE NOT EVEN EATING IT.

I'M SAVING IT FOR A SNACK FOR LATER.

YOU'RE SAVING IT FOR A SNACK?

I'M TAKING IT TO MY ROOM AND...

...OH, WHAT'S WRONG WITH ME? I COULDN'T ENJOY IT KNOWING YOU WERE THAT HUNGRY. ...HERE. TAKE MY RADISH. I WANT YOU TO HAVE MY RADISH.

...REALLY?

I'LL GIVE YOU $25 FOR THAT RADISH.

SOLD!

THINK MUSCLE DEFINITION!

BICEP DEFINITION! TRICEP DEFINITION! QUADRACEP DEFINITION!

NOW TUCK IN THOSE ABDOMINALS, FLEX THOSE PECTORALS, FACE THE MIRROR AND WHAT DO YOU SEE??!

FAT DEFINITION.

AS WE LINE UP FOR OUR FINAL WEIGH-IN, LET ME JUST CAUTION YOU THAT IN DIETING, AS IN LIFE, SUCCESS IS SOMETIMES OUR WORST ENEMY.

FOR SOME DIETERS, LOSING A LITTLE WEIGHT ONLY MAKES THEM REALIZE THEY COULD HAVE LOST THE WEIGHT YEARS AGO, AND HURLS THEM INTO A WHOLE NEW DEPRESSIVE CYCLE OF SELF-LOATHING AND OVEREATING.

TAP TAP

I LOST SEVEN POUNDS!!

STAFF

FOR OTHERS, THIS IS NOT A PROBLEM.

KISS KISS KISS KISS KISS KISS

STAFF

I CAN'T WAIT FOR MY FRIENDS TO SEE THE NEW ME!

JUST REMEMBER... CRASH DIETING HAS SLOWED OUR BODIES' METABOLISM, SO WE'LL TEND TO RE-GAIN WEIGHT EVEN FASTER, CATHY.

ALSO, ALTHOUGH PART OF WHAT WE LOST WAS MUSCLE, ALL OF WHAT WE'LL RE-GAIN WILL BE FAT...AND SINCE FAT TAKES LESS ENERGY TO SUSTAIN, EVEN A TINY GAIN OF NEW FAT WILL MAKE US GAIN EVEN MORE NEW FAT.

PLUS, UNLESS FAT CELLS ARE SURGICALLY REMOVED, THEY'RE IN YOUR BODY FOR LIFE... OUR ONLY HOPE IS TO KEEP OUR NEWLY SHRUNKEN FAT CELLS FROM EXPANDING AND MULTI-PLYING MORE QUICKLY THAN WE CAN KEEP SQUASHING THEM BACK DOWN TO SIZE.

CAN'T THIS PLANE GO ANY FASTER??!!

OUR FAT CELLS ARE DIVIDING.

I DIDN'T EVEN SERVE LUNCH YET.

YOU LOST SEVEN POUNDS IN A WEEK?!

YES... I LIVED ON LETTUCE AND PO-TASSIUM BROTH... I WORKED ON THE MACHINES UNTIL EVERY MUSCLE WAS SCREAMING IN PAIN...

I RAN! SWEATED! CRIED! STARVED!... BUT IT WAS WORTH IT! IT WAS WORTH IT JUST TO HEAR WHAT IRVING SAYS WHEN HE SEES THE NEW ME!!

HI, CATHY. GUESS WHAT? I CUT OUT ONE OF MY EVENING SUNDAES WHILE YOU WERE GONE AND LOST NINE POUNDS!

...AND SHE SAYS WE NEVER HAVE PASSIONATE REUNIONS....

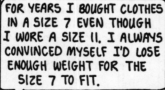

Panel 1:
THAT HOUSE?! NO! ICK!

WHAT DO YOU MEAN, "ICK"? YOU DIDN'T EVEN SEE INSIDE IT YET.

Panel 2:
I WILL **NOT** LIVE IN A HOUSE THAT LOOKS LIKE THAT.

WELL, WE DON'T REALLY KNOW UNTIL WE SEE WHAT'S THERE, DO WE??

Panel 3:
YES. WE KNOW. AND FOR ONCE IN OUR LIVES, WE WANT TO GET TO REJECT SOMETHING JUST ON LOOKS WITHOUT HAVING TO SEARCH FOR INNER BEAUTY! WE **HATE** HOW THAT HOUSE LOOKS! HA, HA! BLEAH!! HA, HA!!

Panel 4:
YOU HURT ITS FEELINGS.

OH, ICK.

Panel 5:
I LOVED THAT HOUSE, MOM!

I LOVED IT TOO, CATHY!

DIDN'T YOU THINK IT WAS A LITTLE SMALL?

YES! TOO SMALL! NO RESALE VALUE!

Panel 6:
BUT THE SMALLNESS MADE IT COZY.

EVERYONE LOVES A COZY HOUSE!

I THINK MORE PEOPLE LIKE BIG HOUSES.

YES! BIGGER IS ALWAYS BETTER!

Panel 7:
MAYBE THAT HOUSE IS TOO BIG FOR ONE PERSON.

YOU'RE RIGHT! TOO BIG!

I THOUGHT YOU THOUGHT IT WAS TOO SMALL.

YES! TOO SMALL! TOO SMALL IN A BIG WAY!

Panel 8:
AAAGH!

IN THE SHORT RUN, I'M DRIVING HER CRAZY. IN THE LONG RUN, SHE'LL THINK OF ME AS "SUPPORTIVE."

Panel 9:
WHEN A MAN LETS A WOMAN WATCH SPORTS WITH HIM ON TV, HE'S LETTING HER INTO A SACRED PART OF HIS WORLD.

Panel 10:
THIS IS WHAT WE LOVE... WHAT WE LIVE FOR! THE FEARLESS DRIVE... INCREDIBLE STRENGTH.. LASER REACTIONS... BRILLIANT TEAMWORK... FINESSE...

Panel 11:
WATCH A MAN'S HEROES UP CLOSE, CATHY, AND YOU'LL SEE EVERYTHING THE MAN IS STRIVING TO BE IN HIS LIFE!

Panel 12:
I WANT YOU TO BE MORE LIKE SPUDS MCKENZIE!

GO HOME.